America

Back on Track

SENATOR
EDWARD M. KENNEDY

America
Back on Track

■ ■ ■ ■ ■

Viking

VIKING
Published by the Penguin Group
Penguin Group (USA) Inc., 375 Hudson Street,
New York, New York 10014, U.S.A.
Penguin Group (Canada), 90 Eglinton Avenue East, Suite 700, Toronto,
Ontario, Canada M4P 2Y3 (a division of Pearson Penguin Canada Inc.)
Penguin Books Ltd, 80 Strand, London WC2R 0RL, England
Penguin Ireland, 25 St. Stephen's Green, Dublin 2, Ireland
(a division of Penguin Books Ltd)
Penguin Books Australia Ltd, 250 Camberwell Road, Camberwell,
Victoria 3124, Australia (a division of Pearson Australia Group Pty Ltd)
Penguin Books India Pvt Ltd, 11 Community Centre,
Panchsheel Park, New Delhi – 110 017, India
Penguin Group (NZ), Cnr Airborne and Rosedale Roads, Albany,
Auckland 1310, New Zealand (a division of Pearson New Zealand Ltd)
Penguin Books (South Africa) (Pty) Ltd, 24 Sturdee Avenue,
Rosebank, Johannesburg 2196, South Africa

Penguin Books Ltd, Registered Offices:
80 Strand, London WC2R 0RL, England

First published in 2006 by Viking Penguin,
a member of Penguin Group (USA) Inc.

1 3 5 7 9 10 8 6 4 2

Copyright © Edward M. Kennedy, 2006
All rights reserved

Graphs by John Del Gaizo

ISBN: 0-670-03764-8

Printed in the United States of America
Set in Adobe Caslon

To Vicki,
Who cares deeply about the direction of our country too
and whose passion for a better America inspires me
each and every day in all I do.

Acknowledgments

In a sense, this book is an outgrowth of many years of Senate debates that have helped crystallize my views on the vital challenges the nation continues to face at home and abroad. Serving the people of Massachusetts as their senator has been the greatest privilege of my life, and I'm very grateful to the many constituents, friends, colleagues in Congress on both sides of the aisle, and past and current staff members who have helped to define and refine these issues in committee sessions, field hearings, and debates on the Senate floor.

As Winston Churchill said, "It has been said that democracy is the worst form of government except all the others that have been tried." Sometimes the process isn't pretty, but free and open debate is the only realistic way to maintain the priceless gift of liberty that the founders of our nation gave us two centuries ago. I have immense respect for all the public servants at every level of government who dedicate their lives to preserving and advancing America's ideals. We may disagree on particular issues, but out of our debates comes a stronger, fairer, and better America. I hope that in the congressional elections in November 2006 a majority of our people will agree with my view that the nation has departed too far from its ideals in too many ways in recent years and that the time has come to put America back on track.

Acknowledgments

The ideas in this book are my own, but I'm very, very grateful to many who have helped in its preparation. My collaborator in this project, Jeff Madrick, the editor of *Challenge Magazine,* is a thoughtful scholar and respected journalist with expertise in a wide variety of policy issues. I've known Jeff for many years and had numerous excellent discussions with him on major issues, and his assistance on this project has been indispensable. We began it nearly a year ago, and we've spent many productive and enjoyable hours together in Washington and on Cape Cod to complete it.

On issues of defense and national security, I consulted a wide variety of experts, and I'm especially grateful to Madeleine Albright, Harold Koh, General William Nash, William Perry, James Steinberg, William vanden Heuvel, Stephen Walt, and General Anthony Zinni.

Special thanks go as well to Robert Ball, Philip Caper, Eamon Kelly, Robert Reich, and Anthony Romero for their thoughtful critiques on various chapters.

Above all, I owe an immense debt of gratitude to my wonderful wife, Vicki, whose constant encouragement, total support, wise counsel, and enduring love inspired me to undertake this project and complete it. I could not have done it without her.

Contents

Acknowledgments   ix

INTRODUCTION: **Seven Challenges**   1

CHAPTER ONE: **Reclaiming Our Constitutional
  Democracy**   18

CHAPTER TWO: **Protecting Our National Security**   45

CHAPTER THREE: **Participating in a Shrinking World**   71

CHAPTER FOUR: **Creating an Economy for All**   102

CHAPTER FIVE: **Guaranteeing Health Care
  for Every American**   127

CHAPTER SIX: **Continuing the March of Progress**   149

CHAPTER SEVEN: **Uniting America**   174

Afterword   198

Bibliographical Note   201

Index   205

America
Back on Track

Introduction: Seven Challenges

It helps in this rapidly changing world to look back, to remind ourselves of where we came from, so we can find a clearer vision of where we must go. As I've looked at the challenges we face in America today, I am certain we can conquer them. I know it. I've seen it. I've lived it. And we can do it again.

We live in a time of remarkable human achievement and progress that would have been almost unimaginable to our ancestors. Not long ago, our optimistic vision of the world seemed to tell us that the sky was the limit. But now, with the breakthroughs in science and technology ranging from the mapping of the human genome to the discovery of new galaxies waiting to be explored, we realize that the sky is just the beginning.

At the same time, we find ourselves sliding back into a world that would have been all too familiar to our ancestors. War and violence, hunger and poverty, injustice and abuse of power are as old as the human race. But they are not an unchangeable result of our DNA. We know from our history and our not too distant past that the right leadership can summon, as President Lincoln said, "the better angels of our nature" and inspire us to meet our challenges and make the world a better

1

place. We can start here at home by putting America back on track to reclaim its legacy of opportunity and possibility.

For me, in a very personal way, recalling the examples and lessons of my own early years has helped me understand the direction I think America must take again.

I grew up in a large Irish Catholic family as the youngest of nine children. By their words, their actions, and their love, our parents instilled in all of us the importance of the ties that bind us together—our faith, our family, and our love of this great country. They inspired in us a curiosity to learn and a desire to leave this world better than we found it.

One of my most vivid childhood memories is of our family gatherings around the table at dinnertime. Conversation was lively and interesting, prompted by questions from my mother and father about events of the day. With nine of us eager to impress our parents as well as one another, it was hard to get a word in unless you had something interesting to say. We learned early that the way to be an active part of dinner conversation was to have read a book, to have learned something new in school, or, as we got older, to have traveled to new places. Our parents opened our nine young minds to the world that way, and it's been a wonderful lifelong gift.

I was also blessed to have had a special relationship with my mother's father, John F. Fitzgerald. Grampa's lively personality, endearing charm, and beautiful singing voice earned him the nickname Honey Fitz. He had a love of people and a way with words that led to his election to the Massachusetts State Senate in 1892 and the United States House of Representatives in 1894, and to his inauguration as mayor of Boston in 1906. As a young schoolboy I was fortunate to be able to spend nearly every Sunday in Boston with Grampa. I was his avid student and he was an eager tutor. He loved people, and he seemed to talk to everyone. I heard stories of how he campaigned for office, riding on the train from Boston to Old Orchard Beach, Maine, where so many Bostonians vacationed. He'd walk through all twelve cars, shaking hands and trading stories, and by the time they reached Maine, Grampa knew almost everyone. Then he'd get right back on the train and come back to Boston with a new group of travelers who were returning home, and he'd do the same thing all over again. That was Grampa. He connected with people and found novel ways to do it wherever he was—in front of the Old North Church, in a hotel while on a vacation in Florida, in the kitchens of Boston restaurants, shaking hands with chefs, waiters, and busboys. He knew how to win votes, and he kept up his outreach to people from all walks of life long after he left office. He was always interested in learning something new, hearing people's concerns, and staying current on the issues that mattered most to them. Grampa talked, but more important, he listened.

He was also a student of history, and he made it come alive for me. "There's Bunker Hill, Teddy. Let me tell you about the battle there." And on he'd go, re-creating the scene for me with his unique enthusiasm. He seemed to know every detail of the American Revolution, but what I remember most was his deep faith in the result of the revolution: the American dream. To him it meant equal opportunity, and opposition to prejudice wherever it existed. As the son of Irish immigrants, he'd suffered from prejudice himself. He told me about the signs in local shop windows that read NO IRISH NEED APPLY. But he also told me how he saw America persevere, overcome bigotry, and create opportunity for these new immigrants. He had fought in those battles himself, and he inspired me to do the same.

In fact, all eight of my great-grandparents reached for that dream. They had come from Ireland to these shores within eighteen months of one another in the middle of the nineteenth century to escape the massive famine in their homeland. They dreamed of finding good jobs, starting their own businesses, and giving their children a decent education. A nation dedicated to equality unleashed the energies of such people, and they loved America because of it. Grampa was determined to continue waging that battle so others could take the same road.

My family's religious views also demanded dedication to the needs and concerns of the least among us, and my parents passed that gift of faith on to all of their children. Every day we prayed at home or in church, and often at both places. My sisters and brothers and I all attended formal classes in religion and received the sacraments in our church. Our parents believed these lessons of faith would mold the people we would become.

At the same time, they believed deeply in freedom of religion, without interference from government. They had endured ethnic and religious prejudice, and they wanted to end it. Freedom to worship in our faith could only be possible if others were free to worship in theirs.

Still, the lessons we drew from our religious faith influenced our values and our vision of what America should be. For me, the most profound message is in the Gospel of Matthew: "For I was hungry and you gave me food, I was thirsty and you gave me drink, a stranger and you welcomed me, naked and you clothed me, ill and you cared for me, in prison and you visited me." Similar themes are found in most of the great books of religion or philosophy. That sense of community and compassion, the belief that we are all in this together, has echoes in every moral system, whether religious or secular, and is at the heart of the great promise of America.

I had just become a teenager when World War II ended, but I was deeply moved by the stories my brother Jack brought home from the war—and by the ultimate sacrifice my brother Joe had made on a highly dangerous mission in the service of our country. I met many of Jack's friends who had fought in the war, and I saw how proud they all were to have been part of something so much larger than themselves.

I was fourteen when Jack ran for Congress in 1946, but I remember what he told me shortly after he took office. He was taking me around Washington, pointing out the different landmarks. He showed me the White House, the Supreme Court, the Library of Congress, and finally the Capitol and the House and Senate office buildings. I loved it. Jack had the same knack as Grampa for bringing history alive. But the thing that is seared in my memory and that has influenced the rest of my life is what my brother said to me at the end of our day of touring. "It's good that you're interested in seeing these buildings, Teddy. But I hope you also take an interest in what goes on inside them."

Jack's words had an impact on me, but I didn't realize how

much until 1954, when the Supreme Court handed down the landmark decision in *Brown v. Board of Education.* The Court declared segregation in the schools to be unconstitutional, and my eyes were opened to the awesome power of our government to create change for the good. I was still in college, but my future path started to become clearer to me. I heeded my brother's advice to take an interest in what happened inside the buildings in Washington, and I began to acquire a deeper understanding of government and its institutions. America worked, I realized, because its three separate but equal branches monitored one another. When two of those branches failed to protect the rights of Americans, the third often rose to the occasion. In the *Brown* decision, the Supreme Court stood up when Congress and the president did not.

The Court's 1954 decision focused the nation's attention on the racial inequality that still plagued America nearly a century after the Civil War. It was a time when Martin Luther King, Jr., began to lead the way forward. He had earned a doctoral degree at Boston University School of Theology in 1955, at a time when I was becoming deeply interested in politics. Although I didn't meet him personally until the 1960s, I was riveted, as was much of the nation, by his unsurpassed eloquence and moral force.

By the time my brother was elected president in 1960, the issue of racial equality had become central to the American agenda. In 1962, I was honored to be elected to represent Massachusetts in the United States Senate and to join with others to be a voice for positive change. I made my maiden speech in the Senate in support of the Civil Rights Act of

1964, and I was proud to be part of the great battle for equality.

For much of my career we were winning the battle, step by step. But it was by no means easy. Violence, tragedy, bloodshed, and loss marred those early years. But Dr. King and the many foot soldiers he inspired had created a powerful nonviolent movement that kept the issue at the forefront of our national discourse. At the national level, President Kennedy and then President Johnson spoke eloquently and directly to the nation about the need for change. We had courageous political leaders who staked their careers and their lives on making America a better and fairer nation—Robert Kennedy, Byron White, Burke Marshall, Nicholas Katzenbach, and Harris Wofford in the Justice Department, to name a few. Mike Mansfield, Hubert Humphrey, Phil Hart, and Everett Dirksen were similar leaders in the Senate. We had judges who understood the real-world implications of their decisions and gave life to the post–Civil War constitutional guarantee of equal protection for all Americans, regardless of the color of their skin. J. Skelly Wright, John Minor Wisdom, Frank M. Johnson, and Earl Warren were just a few of the judicial heroes of the time. We joined together as a nation—Democrats and Republicans, blacks and whites, women and men—to bring meaning to the profound words inscribed in stone over the entrance to the Supreme Court: EQUAL JUSTICE UNDER LAW.

A century after the Civil War ended, we outlawed racial segregation, eliminated the poll tax that had barred many African Americans from voting, guaranteed equal access to public accommodations, outlawed job discrimination because of race or gender, and passed the Fair Housing Act. These were more than simply laws; they affected real people and real lives and bore witness to who we were as Americans and what kind of nation we wanted to be. We showed the world that our young revolutionary nation was still on the march for progress.

We also tackled other pressing issues. These were hard-fought, often brutal battles, to be sure—as highly charged and polarizing as any debate we are having today—but our leaders continued the drumbeat for equality, and we made progress. In 1972 we outlawed discrimination against women in colleges and universities. The next year we passed the Rehabilitation Act as a down payment on ending discrimination against the disabled. In 1975 we banned job discrimination on the basis of age, and in 1990 we passed the Americans with Disabilities Act to give greater protection and access to the full life of our nation to our 40 million brothers and sisters in America who are physically or mentally disabled.

We had also eliminated ethnic quotas on Asian immigrants at a time when only a handful of Asians were allowed to enter the country every year. I was the proud sponsor of the legislation that ended those quotas in 1965, and the enormous contributions of Asian immigrants since that time proves that America is made stronger—not weaker—by our diversity. I strongly support legislation today to keep America open to legal immigrants, to enable them to use their talents and apply their skills in our economy and in all other aspects of our nation's life.

In the midst of all of the racial battles of the 1960s, we also enacted Medicare, guaranteeing good health care for all our senior citizens. Throughout history, respect for the elderly has been the hallmark of every great nation. After all the sacrifices and contributions they have made for their families and our country, no senior citizen in America should be without health care. By passing Medicare we were saying that the care of the elderly reflected our basic values.

As we were taking these major steps to improve the lives of citizens here at home, the nation was also facing enormous foreign policy challenges and threats that were as great as any we are facing today. The Cold War and the dangers of the atomic age put at risk the world as we knew it. Some sought to misuse concerns about safety as an excuse to trample our most fundamental principles. But because of strong leadership, and the willingness of so many to fight for a better country at the same time as we sought a safer world, we were also able to make progress on equality and justice here at home while making great progress in protecting America from threats from abroad. We had leaders who were able to govern from a position of strength, and who challenged us to be a better nation, without stoking the fears of our people.

The rise of the Soviet Union as a superpower and the dawn of the atomic age had required a new definition of national security. We could not look back. We had to look forward. With considerable and contentious public debate, we developed a national consensus in support of containing the expansionist ambitions of the Soviet Union. The policy was a remarkable success, but it required constant foresight and vigilance.

A strong military was equally essential to victory in the Cold War. As a nation we were committed to having the best-trained, best-led troops in the world, with the best equipment and best cutting-edge technology. But we kept our broader focus on what it takes to maintain national security. At home, we worked for equality of education and equality of opportunity for all our citizens. In foreign policy we did not look solely to our armed forces to preserve the peace. We took a much broader worldview and looked toward prevention of conflict as much as toward victory in conflict.

In 1963, with the approval of Congress, President Kennedy signed the first nuclear test ban treaty with Nikita Khrushchev of the Soviet Union. That early initiative and the later efforts of President Johnson laid the groundwork for the subsequent signing of key arms-control treaties. Before those treaties took effect, commentators had routinely predicted that there would soon be twenty to twenty-five nations with nuclear-weapons capability. In fact, today there are fewer than ten. Prevention, containment, and foresight worked.

Americans respond to challenges, and they also respond to strong leadership. In 1957, after the Soviets launched *Sputnik*, we responded by doubling the federal education budget to increase the number of college students graduating in science. In 1961, President Kennedy challenged the nation to put a man on the moon by the end of the decade so that space would not be filled with weapons of death but used instead to advance the causes of freedom and knowledge for the whole world. In an address on the space program at Rice University in 1962, he cited William Bradford, the founder of the Plymouth Bay Colony, who said in 1630 that "all great and honorable actions are accompanied with great difficulties, and both must be enterprised and overcome with answerable courage." With that reference my brother tapped into the essential qualities of the American spirit—courage, honor, and ingenuity—and the nation responded. He didn't sugarcoat the difficulties we faced. He inspired us to rise to the challenge and to reach new heights of human achievement.

In that same spirit, he announced the formation of the Peace Corps. Within weeks of taking office in 1961 he called on the American people "to sacrifice their energies and time and toil to the cause of world peace and human progress" by helping foreign countries meet their growing need for skilled workers. As he stated:

> Life in the Peace Corps will not be easy. . . . But if the life will not be easy, it will be rich and satisfying. For every young American who participates in the Peace Corps—who works in a foreign land—will know that he or she is sharing in the great common task of bringing to man that decent way of life which is the foundation of freedom and a condition of peace.

Inspired by President Kennedy and the leadership of Sargent Shriver, young men and women by the hundreds and then the thousands answered the call. When I met with a group of volunteers on the fifth anniversary of the Peace Corps, I was deeply moved by the nearly unanimous reason they gave for joining: "No one had ever asked us to do something for someone else." Like my brother and his friends after World War II, they were proud to be a part of something bigger than themselves: America at its best; Americans at their best.

In an earlier time, in the wake of a devastating war, we had seen the success of the Marshall Plan when we provided financial aid to rebuild the countries of both our allies and the enemies we had vanquished. It was a strong, bold, and magnanimous policy that paid off dramatically in maintaining peace and expanding trade. We benefited from the new markets these rebuilt countries created for our goods and the new products they made for our consumers. We refused to be limited by anger or prejudice against the enemies we had fought so bitterly. Instead, we looked to the future with a rationality that strived to make us safer and more prosperous by making our enemies our friends. Again, it was America at its best.

I do not underestimate the problems we faced in those days. The difficulties were enormous and at times seemed insurmountable. The Cold War raged, the Vietnam War escalated, leaders were murdered, young people died, cities burned. Somehow we found a way to keep going forward. We can find that way again.

Always in the past, and often against large odds, our people have risen to meet the great challenges of the day, and I have no doubt the American people are ready to do so again. But we need bold and inspired leadership. We need to reclaim the American spirit of courage and honor and ingenuity, and set our course anew.

I do not recite these facts from our past to suggest that we should go back to the "good old days." I cite them instead as inspiration and examples of what can be accomplished in even the most difficult and challenging times when we all come together as a community and as a nation. We must accept the responsibility to meet the challenges in our country and in our world. It is the only realistic way to continue our progress so that America's best years are still to come.

The challenges confronting us go well beyond the war in Iraq or the dangers of terrorism, as important as those issues are. There are security threats at home and abroad, from foreign enemies and their sympathizers as well as from the age-old enemies poverty and injustice, and the abuse of power here at home. We must face these problems without fear and with honesty and reason. But face them we must, because they affect almost every aspect of our lives and they go to the heart of what it means to be American.

Our leaders today do not look at these challenges directly, openly, and honestly. Far from it. It seems at times that our democracy is in disarray.

We can change direction, and that process begins by defining and meeting the challenges. That is always when America is at its best. Each time we are challenged we exceed ourselves. But today we are not being called upon by our leaders to solve our critical problems. We are not being asked to sacrifice. We are not given the truth about the problems we confront. After more than four decades in the Senate, I have never felt a greater need to call attention to these issues and to do so without scare tactics but with respect for the courage, integrity, and ingenuity that have always defined the true American spirit.

Would we create Social Security today? Would we pass Medicare? Would we enact the great civil rights laws of the 1960s, the Civil Rights Act of 1964, the Voting Rights Act of

1965, and the Fair Housing Act of 1968? Would we persuade the world to accept a nuclear arms control treaty?

I believe we will do what is necessary today if we have leaders who make clear what our choices are and who trust the American people with the truth about these challenges. With real leadership, we'll unite around our great principles and our spirit of community, and together we'll prevail.

I am writing this book because I believe Americans are ready—indeed, eager—to meet our nation's greatest challenges. To start that essential process I set forth seven critical challenges. Each reflects a modern test of our oldest principles. But each also offers us a chance to join with the great generations that preceded us in fulfilling America's promise.

The first challenge is to reclaim our constitutional democracy and keep it vital for the future.

The Founding Fathers established separate executive, judicial, and legislative branches in order to create a system of checks and balances that would protect Americans from tyranny. That system is under threat today. The executive branch has increasingly asserted its right to act in secrecy and to ignore laws passed by Congress. The courts have not yet stepped up to the challenges posed by these unprecedented claims of presidential power, and the majority in Congress has chosen uncritical support for the president instead of meeting their constitutional duty to oversee and check executive power. The judicial branch has increasingly substituted its judgment for that of Congress on issues of national importance. The result is a federal system that is dangerously unbalanced. We must insist on a return to the Framers' vision of three branches that respect and check one another.

The second challenge is to develop a new definition of national security for a changed world.

I believe that the tragedy of September 11, 2001, will produce the next great generation of Americans, just as the attack on Pearl Harbor summoned a new generation to defend our country and the world. But today's leaders are looking backward, not forward. They recognize only one method of leadership—military power—while ignoring diplomacy, economic development, and the protection of human rights. They fail to recognize that poverty and national humiliation are as dangerous to our security as any weapon. We need to return to the most effective ways America has influenced nations throughout the world in the past: by offering a helping hand and abiding by our deepest principles—rather than jettisoning them in the name of national security.

The third challenge is to participate fully in a shrinking world.

We now live on a planet where the products we buy may be made in distant lands, our medical records stored in computers half a world away, and vital research carried out in educated corners of the poorest nations. America must respond to globalization by preparing every man, woman, and child to compete successfully in this new world. We must commit ourselves to excellence in education for all and invest the resources needed to reach that goal. Each past generation of Americans has broadened educational opportunities for its youth, and the global economy demands that we do no less today.

The fourth challenge is to achieve an economy that works for all, not just for a privileged few.

The incomes of Americans are as unequal today as they were under President Hoover. The inequality of wealth is even worse—and likely to deepen. As the opening words of the Constitution proclaim, "a more perfect union" is dedicated to "the general welfare"—not prosperity for some and poverty for others.

The fifth challenge is to provide health care to every American.

One of the most jarring consequences of inequality in America is that we are capable of providing first-rate medical care but fail to make it available to many millions of our people. The solution seems as simple as it is obvious, and it is well grounded in the American experience: Medicare for all.

The sixth challenge is to resume the march of progress toward equal opportunity for all.

Despite the many gains, there is still unacceptable prejudice against people of color. There is bigotry against too many others as well, and in important areas we have moved backward in recent years. The evidence of bias against women in the workforce is undeniable, and so is the evidence of bias against gays and lesbians. We cannot allow the march of progress to come to a halt or to shift into reverse.

The seventh challenge is to restore our basic values and reunite our nation.

We hear about our values all the time these days. We are told that we are divided over our most basic beliefs. I do not believe that is true. We have differences of opinion, because we pride ourselves on our pluralism. But there is much more that unites us. We share a profound commitment to basic rights for all—rights to life and liberty, to opportunity, to a decent education, to a job. We believe in fairness and honesty in business. We believe in a free press eager to speak truth to power. We believe that the government cannot tell us whom we can marry or where we can worship or intrude on any of our other important personal and family decisions. With so much to unite us, we must join together in rejecting those who coarsen our political system and divide us for their own political purposes.

These challenges are daunting. But if we ask our people to meet them, they will respond with the same energy and commitment that Americans have always shown when their leaders trust them and lead. Together, we can put America back on track.

CHAPTER ONE

Reclaiming Our Constitutional Democracy

Our founders created a brilliant and inspired constitutional democracy that, tragically, is under assault today. I believe we must take action now to reclaim the essential freedoms of our democracy, which President Lincoln so eloquently described as "the last, best hope of earth."

The battle that many of us are waging for our fundamental way of governing is sometimes portrayed as a mere difference between opposing political points of view. But it is so much more than that. It is a battle for America's heart and soul.

We have leaders today who admit to ignoring specific laws passed by Congress, and they vow to continue doing so. They violate the Constitution—especially the Bill of Rights—and tell us they are making us safer. But how can we be safer when our fundamental rights are ignored or abused under the guise of executive prerogatives? That kind of unchecked power is precisely the reason our ancestors declared their independence and fought the American Revolution. It is directly contrary to the mandates of our Constitution, which is the best reflection of the true values of our nation and the true will of our people.

Many of our actions as a nation in recent years offend the basic ideals of freedom and decency that we have so proudly and rightly proclaimed to the world for so long. These ideals have always been our greatest export and have encouraged and influenced the growth of democracy in other lands for generations. We must come together again to reclaim our legacy of liberty here at home and regain our position of positive leadership in the world.

The genius of our Constitution is that it establishes a government carefully designed to protect the hard-won freedoms of the American people. Those protections are as relevant and as necessary today as they were in 1787, when the Constitution was signed. The founders believed that the best safeguard against the abuse of power is the separation of the powers of government into three distinct branches, with each serving as a watchdog over the other two. We must never forget the history of this founding document. The people of our new republic had just fought a difficult and bloody war to gain independence from a repressive and tyrannical king, and they believed that a separation rather than a concentration of powers was essential to the preservation of liberty.

So our founders created a legislative branch—the House of Representatives and the Senate—to pass laws; an executive branch, led by the president, to implement the laws; and a judicial branch, led by the Supreme Court, to resolve disputes about the laws. As part of this system of checks and balances the president has the power to veto legislation passed by Congress, but Congress has the power to override that veto if a two-thirds majority of the House and Senate agrees. The Supreme Court under Chief Justice John Marshall properly assumed the power to declare laws unconstitutional in 1803, in

Marbury v. Madison, but if the people disagree with the courts or wish to modify the Constitution, they have the power to amend it, as has been done twenty-seven times, including the first ten amendments, the Bill of Rights.

For more than two centuries this brilliant system has served our nation well, because our founders vested the real power in the hands of the people. As the Constitutional Convention ended, Benjamin Franklin was asked what he had wrought, and he answered: "A republic—if you can keep it." Our founders knew it would not be easy, but they believed in the American spirit and the willingness of the people to make the sacrifices necessary to preserve their freedoms.

Today, however, that crucial system of checks and balances is being abused, and as patriotic Americans we must join together and take action to preserve our freedoms.

I am particularly concerned about the blurring of the lines between the powers of the executive and legislative branches, and even between the judicial and executive branches.

The president is allocating power to himself in dangerous ways, and with both houses of Congress controlled by the president's party, there is far too little oversight and far too few attempts to rein in extravagant exercises of power. Indeed, the Republican president and the Republican-controlled Congress act so often in lockstep today that they make a mockery of the founding principle of separation of powers. All too often Congress is willing simply to rubber-stamp the wishes of the president, even if it means violating long-standing congressional rules, traditions, and basic constitutional responsibilities. Most dangerous, I believe, is the acquiescence by Congress in the president's demand for unprobing acceptance of his agenda, even on issues as critically important to the nation as war and peace.

Some suggest that this kind of unanimous, partisan support for the president is simply a reflection of his strong leadership and the legislators' 100 percent belief in his agenda. If that is so, then why not trust the American people to have open and honest debates on these issues? Why not have real congressional hearings on the most important issues of the day? Why not permit Democrats to participate actively in the conference committees that are traditionally used to reconcile the differences in bills passed by the House and the Senate? Today, those rules of Congress have been thrown aside. To get his way the president requires the Republican leadership in Congress to discipline their party members to vote his way, reject contrary views, and even limit open discussion. That's not leadership; it's bullying. These practices are contrary to the American spirit of government, and we must shine light on them so that the people can know the truth.

The administration has also repeatedly appointed to high offices cronies and friends who have no experience or competence in their area of responsibility. Lobbyists have unusual access to the White House and Congress. Money now talks far too loudly in Washington and in elections. The price the nation is paying is the stunning culture of corruption that has infected the administration and its allies in Congress.

Perhaps the greatest threat to our constitutional democracy is the Bush administration's extreme view about the source and scope of its war powers and about its unilateral right to ignore laws passed by Congress. Behind closed doors the administration has devised controversial legal justifications for unspeakable torture, ignoring both congressional acts and court precedent, while at the same time doing irreparable damage to the image of our nation, which was once revered around the world for its respect for human rights. There is more and more evidence that our government has been sending prisoners to foreign nations to be tortured. Even though Article I, Section 8 of the Constitution expressly provides that it is the Congress that has the authority to "make Rules concerning Captures on Land and Water," the president and his advisers—without court or congressional approval—have decided that the president has almost plenary, unchecked power as the commander in chief of the military to decide whether or not he will follow laws passed by Congress under its constitutional power. They have also decided that he can hide his noncompliance with the law as a matter of national security. Based on such theories, President Bush has claimed authority to spy on the American people without a court order, even though the Foreign Intelligence Surveillance Act, which I was deeply involved in passing in 1978, expressly requires judicial authorization for such searches, and even sets up a secret court to expedite its proceedings. The president and administration officials have tried to advance several different justifications for warrantless searches of American citizens, but their bottom line argument seems to be that the president can do what he wants as commander in chief. He sometimes refuses even to take his requests to the secret court. That is precisely the kind of abuse of power that our founders intended to prevent when they wrote the Constitution. The notion that our Constitution permits one branch of government to do whatever it wants, in secret, without any judicial or congressional oversight in time of war is a dangerous and ill-conceived arrogation of power, and we must take action to stop it.

The right to privacy of our citizens is protected by the Constitution, but we have a leadership today that acts as if its official actions—rather than individual Americans—are covered by the right to privacy.

Undermining the Role of Congress

In 2003, many of us were determined to add prescription drug coverage to Medicare. Drug costs for the elderly had long been rising to levels that many could not afford, and action by Congress was overdue. A bipartisan group of senators produced a realistic plan that the Senate approved.

With the support and encouragement of the president, however, the Republican-led House of Representatives produced a very different bill. Rather than strengthen Medicare and use funds to benefit the elderly, the House bill used federal money to subsidize private insurance companies and gave tax breaks to those who needed them the least. But most dangerous, the bill contained a demonstration program designed—as part of a stealth agenda—to privatize Medicare

The tradition of Congress is to iron out such differences in conference committees of House and Senate members. The House leaders, however, stacked the deck. In what has become a common tactic under these leaders, Democrats—who had serious disagreements with the House version of the bill—were not allowed to participate in the negotiations. Through strong-arm tactics and abuse of the rules, the House Republican leaders produced exactly the bill they wanted in the conference committee. Once the conference committee's bill reached the House floor, however, they couldn't produce enough votes to pass it in the fifteen minutes usually allotted for a roll-call vote. But the Republican leaders were not deterred. They abruptly changed long-standing House rules and kept the vote open for more than three hours in the middle of the night while they twisted arms until they changed enough votes to win passage of their bill. Added controversy erupted when a Republican congressman from Michigan revealed that he had been promised $100,000 from business interests for his son's election campaign if he voted for the bill.

The bill passed by five votes, but it was not democracy at work. Instead, it was a stark example of the White House and congressional leadership steamrolling democracy. When word of the arm twisting and multihour vote became public, I was reminded of a time in 1987 when the Democrats, who were then in charge of the House, kept a vote open for ten extra minutes. Dick Cheney was the Republican House leader at the time, and he angrily claimed it was "the most arrogant, heavy-handed abuse of power in the ten years I've been here." As vice president in 2003, however, he apparently was no longer concerned about the "arrogant, heavy-handed abuse of power."

The lockstep mentality of Congress and the White House is also apparent in how unified Republican voting has become. According to voting records, Republican Party unity in Congress reached an all-time high in 2003, followed by a close second in 2004. This abrogation of the independence of Congress from the executive is contrary to the fundamental concepts of our constitutional democracy.

The Bush administration and Congress are behaving more like the prime minister and parliament in a parliamentary system, where the prime minister by definition is not independent of the legislative body. Instead, the party with the most seats in parliament puts together a government led by the prime minister, who is the leader of the party. There is lockstep approval of the prime minister's agenda by the majority party because they are, in essence, one and the same. But there is one glaring difference between the way this adminstration and a parliamentary system function. In the latter, the prime minister can be challenged by a vote of no confidence, forcing him to resign or call a new election. In our country the president is in office for four years, until the next scheduled election, even if his party loses its majority in Congress, and even if the people have "no confidence" in him.

The power of Congress has been usurped in other serious ways. A controversial redistricting plan was passed by the Texas legislature in 2003, under the direction of House Majority Leader Tom DeLay, to win more Republican seats for the House by redrawing the boundaries of congressional districts so that minorities could not dominate them. The districts had been redrawn already, after the 2000 census, as is the usual practice every ten years, but DeLay saw an opportunity to force a more Republican-friendly redistricting plan through the Republican-controlled Texas legislature. The politically charged redistricting plan was so bitterly contested that the Democratic members of the state legislature suddenly left the state by plane to prevent a final vote. Republicans threatened to have them rounded up by state police, and DeLay ordered the Federal Aviation Administration to track the plane to find the missing state legislators. He was later rebuked for his actions by the House Ethics Committee, but the redistricting plan went forward. Because of the gerrymandered districts it created, DeLay and House Republicans were able to gain additional seats to strengthen their majority in Congress. That's more than "just politics," as some have tried to argue. It's a shameful abuse of power.

In late 2005, information became public that even though career civil rights attorneys in the Justice Department had concluded that under federal law the redistricting plan violated the rights of minority voters in Texas, they were overruled by Bush-appointed senior officials in the department. In a hopeful sign, however, we also learned that the Supreme Court agreed to hear a case challenging the legality of the abusive redistricting plan.

The Justice Department's involvement in the political agenda of the Bush administration and Republican-led Congress was not limited to the Texas case. More recently, after the state of Georgia enacted legislation to require a government-issued identification card for all voters, career civil rights lawyers in the Justice Department concluded that the requirement violated federal law because it unlawfully restricted the right to vote of low-income Americans, particularly African Americans. In a repeat of the Texas redistricting case, the political appointees again overruled the career attorneys in the department and allowed the plan to go forward. The hypocrisy is obvious. An administration that loudly trumpets its support for democracy around the world refuses to support it in its own backyard. A highly regarded career lawyer left the department, frustrated that partisan politics was overruling the rule of law and the official who overruled her was rewarded by President Bush with an appointment to the federal commission. The Eleventh Circuit Court of Appeals invalidated the new rule, holding that the law did indeed violate the Voting Rights Act, just as the career lawyers had advised.

The Bush administration is also weakening agencies that enforce congressional laws. It has cut dozens of positions at the Occupational Safety and Health Administration and reduced its budget significantly. It has opposed including ergonomic injuries on the list of safety violations for which businesses should be held responsible. It has seriously weakened the enforcement of environmental rules by the Environmental Protection Agency and rolled back existing regulations significantly. It has exerted political pressure on the Food and Drug Administration and weakened the Equal Employment Opportunity Commission. The nation's chief executive has a constitutional responsibility to execute the laws, but in this context, "execute" means implement, not kill.

Secrecy

It is difficult to assess how secret an administration is, but I have never seen an administration so determined to keep important information from Congress and the people. An un-precedented level of secrecy characterizes far too many actions of the administration. This extraordinary secrecy—executive orders declaring information off-limits; large numbers of documents classified as top secret without a compelling national security reason; secret courts and detentions; secret memoranda authorizing torture; secret eavesdropping on American citizens; secret meetings with corporate leaders who want policies favorable to their interests—is a major threat to our democracy. The administration obviously finds traditional oversight and openness repugnant. But information is the basis of our freedoms and an important check on the abuse of power. In a successful democracy, Congress and the executive branch must be open and accountable. Under the Bush administration, however, openness and accountability have been replaced by secrecy, evasion of responsibility, and even deceit.

We know from experience that sunshine is a powerful disinfectant that can help eliminate corruption and abuse of power in government. When the people can see what is happening, they can hold their leaders accountable at the ballot box. Our founders understood the realities of human nature when they wrote checks and balances into the Constitution. As expressed in "Federalist 51," one of the brilliant essays written by the Founders to explain the new Constitution:

> But what is government itself, but the greatest of all reflections on human nature? If men were angels, no government would be necessary. If angels were to govern men, neither external nor internal controls on government would be necessary. In framing a government which is to be administered by

28

men over men, the great difficulty lies in this: You must first enable the government to control the governed; and in the next place oblige it to control itself. A dependence on the people is no doubt the primary control on the government, but experience has taught mankind the necessity of auxiliary precautions.

If a government shrouds its actions in secrecy, it is able to act without any controls at all. Neither the people nor the other branches of government will be able to halt the excesses of power if they are hidden from view. The result is a government run amok, with no accountability whatever.

We still do not know the truth about the intelligence used by President Bush to make the decision to go to war in Iraq. The administration continues to withhold that key information. Cabinet officers and other officials appear before major congressional committees for only a brief time. The administration nominates candidates to the judiciary and refuses to give the Senate the same the information the president used in making the nomination. Relying on claims of privilege, the administration uses secrecy to prevent the Senate from exercising its constitutional obligation of advice and consent. The vice president met in secret with oil industry leaders to draft major energy legislation and flagrantly refused to disclose which corporate interests helped write the bill.

When a president and an administration go to such extremes to conduct their activities in secret, they are abusing the power delegated to them by the people through the Constitution, and they must be called to account.

No one disputes the necessity of avoiding public disclosure

of information critical to our national security. But since 9/11 the Bush administration has classified unprecedented amounts of information. The objective is to avoid independent evaluation. At a hearing in the summer of 2004 the director of the government's Information Security Oversight Office testified, "It is no secret that the government classifies too much information. Too much classification unnecessarily impedes effective information-sharing." A deputy undersecretary of defense for counterintelligence and security said that as much as half of all classified information is classified unnecessarily.

Last year a record 15 million documents were classified by the Bush administration at a cost of more than $7 billion. Many were classified under newly invented categories that have fewer requirements for classification. The administration argues that such secrecy is necessary to win the war on terrorism. But the Report of the 9/11 Commission found that excessive government secrecy had hurt U.S. intelligence capability even before 9/11. "Secrecy stifles oversight, accountability, and information sharing," the report said.

The commissioners understood this truth from their own experience. In July 2003, the commission's cochairmen, Thomas Kean and Lee Hamilton, complained publicly that the administration had failed to provide requested information. Later that year, after repeated requests were denied, the commission subpoenaed information from the Department of Defense and the Federal Aviation Administration. In the following months, the administration repeatedly denied access to presidential documents important to the commission's investigation, until the public outcry grew loud enough to persuade the administration to relent. Key members of the administration balked at testifying to Congress, until public opinion again forced them to come before congressional committees.

The secrecy of the administration also manifests itself in other ways. If the president had campaigned on a platform of eliminating environmental protections and safeguards for public health, voters would have been able to decide whether they wanted a president with such an agenda. As we know, the president did not espouse that kind of platform during either of his campaigns. If he had, he would have lost votes, and given the closeness of both elections, he might well have been defeated. But he did not make these unpopular proposals part of his campaign; they became part of a stealth agenda once he took office. What the president couldn't do politically through the front door of open debate he tried to accomplish through the back door of secrecy. The administration has placed appointees in charge of agencies whose responsibility is to carry out the laws passed by Congress, but the appointees have undermined that responsibility and weakend the agencies' missions in areas ranging from the relaxing of long-standing restrictions on protection of the federal forests to reducing government requirements for tuberculosis testing.

Other important examples exist of the Bush administration unjustifiably keeping information from Congress and the American people.

■ The president's intelligence briefings on Iraq still have not been made public as I write this, despite the efforts of many in Congress to obtain them. The president has repeatedly

31

stated that members of Congress who voted to allow him to go to war had access to the same intelligence the administration had. But Congress clearly did not have access to the so-called "PDB" documents, the Presidential Daily Briefings that the president receives each morning.

■ In May 2001, Vice President Cheney's energy task force issued its report recommending greater oil and gas drilling to solve our energy problems. In light of his former employment at Halliburton, the recommendation was hardly astonishing. What was astonishing was the vice president's refusal to identify the people and groups who helped write the policy. In June that year the Government Accountability Office, the nonpartisan investigative arm of Congress, requested information on the task force after press reports that campaign contributors had had special access while the public was shut out. The GAO request was clear. It asked, "Who serves on this task force; what information is being presented to the task force and by whom is it being given; and . . . the costs involved in the gathering of the facts." The task force wrote the nation's energy policy, so it was an eminently reasonable request, but the administration refused to comply. In contrast, when President Clinton's task forces on health care and on China trade were investigated by the GAO, the Clinton administration turned over detailed information on them. Under the Bush administration, for the first time in its eighty-year history, the GAO was forced to file suit to obtain the requested information. Unfortunately, the court sided with the administration, and the GAO's investigative oversight authority was reduced. The administration's position turned out to be technically legal, but that did not make it right.

■ The pattern of withholding information from members of Congress on administration nominations is especially disturbing. In 2003, Miguel Estrada was nominated for a federal judgeship. Senators requested legal memoranda he had written as assistant solicitor general, and the request was denied. In 2004, Alberto Gonzales was nominated to be attorney general. Senators requested memoranda he authorized on the administration's policy on torture, but the request was denied. In 2005, John Bolton was nominated to be ambassador to the United Nations. Senators requested documents to determine if he had acted appropriately in his previous position, but the request was denied.

■ Cabinet officials have been reluctant to make themselves available to congressional committees. When they do, the time they spend, even before major committees, is highly restricted. Our democracy requires more accountability than this.

■ In one of the most brazen abuses of power, the administration withheld cost estimates of its Medicare prescription drug bill before it was enacted in 2003. The estimates showed that the costs would be $100 billion higher than the administration had claimed, but the information was withheld because of fears that the honest number would cause too many members of Congress to oppose the bill. Administration officials even threatened to fire Medicare's chief actuary, Richard Foster, "so fast his head would spin" if he informed Congress of the real estimate.

▪ In 2003, the Food and Drug Administration kept secret a report that children on antidepressants were twice as likely to be involved in suicide-related behavior. The agency also prevented the author of the study—its own expert on the issue—from presenting his findings to an FDA advisory committee. As Dr. Joseph Glenmullen, a Harvard psychiatrist, has said, "Evidence that they're suppressing a report like this is an outrage, given the public health and safety issues at stake. . . . For the FDA to issue an ambiguous warning when they had unambiguous data like this is an outrage."

Finally, we must also recognize that the administration's desire for absolute secrecy goes beyond simply refusing to make documents public—it does not want any disagreements over its views aired in public. They don't hesitate to punish whistle-blowers, especially those who disagree with their policy on Iraq. The case of retired diplomat Joseph Wilson is a prime example of their despicable tactics. An expert on Africa and the Middle East, Wilson had served with distinction under the first President Bush and President Clinton; as a senior official in the U.S. embassy in Baghdad during the first Gulf war in 1991, columnists Robert Novak and Rowland Evans wrote that he had shown "the stuff of heroism" by risking his life to shelter eight hundred Americans at the embassy to protect them from Saddam Hussein.

In 2002, the CIA sent Wilson to Niger to verify administration claims that Iraq was buying uranium from Niger to use in nuclear weapons. He found no credible evidence to support the claim and wrote a report saying so. Nevertheless, the administration continued to make the allegation, culminating in the notorious "sixteen words" in the president's 2003 State of the Union address: "The British Government has learned that Saddam Hussein recently sought significant quantities of uranium from Africa." When Wilson went public disputing that statement, administration officials tried to undermine his credibility by suggesting he had been sent on the mission only because his wife, Valerie Plame, had recommended him. Plame herself was an undercover officer of the CIA, but her identity was cruelly leaked to the press by the administration to punish her husband and her cover was blown.

In a further blatant move, the administration also took retaliatory action against General Eric Shinseki, the army chief of staff during the prewar planning for the invasion of Iraq. General Shinseki stated publicly that the United States would need at least 250,000 troops on the ground to stabilize postwar Iraq. The adminstration had no intention of committing such a large force, and General Shinseki was overruled. But that was not enough. Angered by his dissent, the administration forced him to resign from his position more than a year before his scheduled retirement.

In yet another case, the UN arms control inspectors searching for evidence of Saddam Hussein's weapons of mass destruction in Iraq were severely ridiculed. Had they been heeded, war could have been avoided, and a more constructive policy to fight terrorism and limit Hussein's power could have been adopted.

As these examples show all too clearly, the administration's commitment to unprecedented secrecy in government and its heavy-handed repression of dissent are contrary to the very essence of our constitutional democracy and to common decency too.

Torture, Secrecy, and Executive Power

America's most shameful embarrassment in many years was the discovery that our troops were torturing prisoners in Iraq. The nation was repelled by these practices and shamed before the world, the insurgency in Iraq became harder to defeat, and the larger war against terrorism became harder to win.

Torture is alien to everything we stand for. The Bill of Rights unequivocally forbids "cruel and unusual punishments," and these words were chosen well. Our founders were determined to end repression and persecution—to free themselves from tyranny and make certain that the practices of dictators would never be used by our leaders.

Torture has never before been an issue that divided Republicans and Democrats. It has always been an issue with a broad consensus in America; it was President Reagan who signed the international treaty against torture in 1988. The Senate Foreign

Relations Committee, led by Republican Senator Jesse Helms of North Carolina and Democratic Senator Claiborne Pell of Rhode Island, voted 10–0 to approve the treaty in 1990. The first President Bush and President Clinton supported its ratification, which was finally achieved in 1994.

Our nation also subscribes to Article 5 of the Universal Declaration of Human Rights, which states that "no one shall be subjected to torture or to cruel, inhuman or degrading treatment or punishment," words obviously chosen to outlaw horrific practices that some could argue did not meet the precise definition of torture.

When news of torture in Abu Ghraib prison in Iraq and other areas came to light, the Bush administration stalled. It refused to provide answers or documents. It refused to hold anyone but lower level military personnel accountable. Instead, it sought to convince America and the world that the abhorrent practices were the work of "a few bad apples."

But unknown to Congress and the American people at that time, the administration had requested a legal memorandum in 2002 on the use of torture. It is one of the most appalling documents in American history, and it became the legal justification for authorizing the use of interrogation techniques that clearly cross the line into torture in spite of our treaty obligation. It remained secret for two years, and was withdrawn by the administration only after it was leaked to the press in 2004.

The memorandum was prepared by then assistant attorney general Jay Bybee of the Office of Legal Counsel in the Department of Justice, and was addressed to President Bush's chief counsel in the White House, Alberto Gonzales, who has since become attorney general. Bybee himself was later appointed to a lifetime federal judgeship. The memorandum claims that torture is forbidden only if the pain inflicted is equivalent to that "accompanying serious physical injury, such as organ failure, impairment of bodily functions or even death."

Under this restrictive definition many of the horrid practices we decried under Saddam Hussein would have been allowed, such as suffocation, ripping out fingernails, and burning victims with hot irons. The memorandum also claimed that President Bush had extraordinary powers as commander in chief to request such practices. Astonishingly, the memorandum stated that Congress had no authority to regulate interrogations by the military, because to do so would violate the president's constitutional powers as commander in chief.

Dean Harold Koh of Yale Law School, a highly respected legal scholar who served in the administrations of both President Reagan and President Clinton, called the Bybee memorandum "the most clearly legally erroneous opinion" he had ever read.

But under George Bush it became executive branch policy. It asserts that U.S. officials can use torture without being held liable under the federal statute that criminalizes torture. It is consistent with other claims for executive power supported by John Yoo, a former Justice Department lawyer and now a professor of law at the University of California at Berkeley who has written extensively about what is called the "unitary executive," a theory of presidential power that many legal scholars repudiate. Yet President Bush has cited this theory in recent years to justify his policies.

Secrecy is at the heart of this abuse of power. The Bybee memorandum only became public after the Abu Ghraib practices were disclosed. It was renounced and replaced by a new memo a few days before the Senate began its hearings on the nomination of Alberto Gonzales to be attorney general.

In an open government, such insults to our nation's values would never have occurred. We would make important legal documents public unless they are of paramount importance for national security. The Office of Legal Counsel, a highly regarded arm of the Justice Department, would be free of politics.

The claims of presidential prerogative pushed by Bush administration lawyers are outrageous and undermine both our Constitution and our values. To this day, those responsible for such torture have not been held accountable. The administration has also stonewalled requests for information on its policy of "rendition," in which prisoners are flown to secret camps in other nations where torture is highly likely.

At the end of 2005, after first threatening to veto it, President Bush finally agreed to a bill, sponsored by Senator John McCain, restricting torture. The worst of this tragic episode seemed to be over. But it wasn't. President Bush issued a devious detailed statement at the time he signed the bill into law, ordering the executive branch to ignore provisions that in his view conflicted with his powers as president. Any lawyer worth his salt could make an argument like that for a client, but no president worth his salt should seek it or accept it.

If the president had abided by his responsibility to make information on this drastic policy known, one of the great shames in the nation's history might have been avoided, and many precious lives spared. Legal opinions of major importance should always be made public, barring serious national security concerns. Above all, though, the president must obey the law. He's the president, not the king.

The Independence of the Judicial Branch

The major current battleground of the battle to preserve the constitutional separation of powers is the Supreme Court. Its independence is at the core of our democracy. Half a century ago, when the president and Congress failed to act adequately against racial discrimination in America, the Supreme Court took up this struggle for justice, and in one of its all-time great decisions outlawed school segregation. In the 1960s, when two presidents and Congress at last took decisive action to bring greater equality to America, the Supreme Court and the lower courts confirmed that the legislation passed by Congress and signed by the president was constitutional.

It is imperative to maintain respect for the laws and the role of the courts that have been vital to the progress of the nation. But today, the independence of the judicial branch and the laws passed that made possible so much progress toward equal rights for all are in danger of being undone. A prevailing myth, encouraged by President Bush, claims that the Supreme Court under Chief Justice Rehnquist practiced judicial restraint. The president says that he seeks only to maintain such restraint through his judicial appointments by choosing judges who will not make law. Nothing could be further from the truth. Under

Chief Justice Rehnquist the Supreme Court overturned more than three dozen laws passed by Congress since 1995. Many of these decisions weakened the power of Congress to make binding laws for the nation. Instead, a narrow ideologized majority of the Court was shifting more and more power to the states.

The validity of federal power arises from the Constitution itself, but its modern affirmation occurred under President Franklin D. Roosevelt. In the preceding decades and the early years of FDR's administration, an extremely conservative Supreme Court repeatedly struck down measures enacted by both Congress and state legislatures to remedy the economic abuses of the time. The Supreme Court ruled against the minimum wage and maximum hour laws, against prohibitions on child labor, against protections of consumers from defective products, and against regulations to prevent corporate abuses. In fact, this was arguably the most "activist" period in our judicial history. The justices were activists in protecting the economic status quo and denying the power of Congress to change it, and their rulings were serious setbacks for millions of working families of that era. This reactionary judicial trend reached its height with the invalidation of several major pieces of New Deal legislation in the early1930s by a closely divided Court.

Finally, an exasperated President Roosevelt attempted to "pack the Court" by increasing the number of justices from nine to fifteen. The plan failed in Congress, but only after one of the conservative justices altered his position—in what has been called "the switch in time that saved nine"—and agreed that the commerce clause of the Constitution gives Congress broad authority over activities that affect the national economy.

41

Between 1937 and 1995 not a single congressional enactment based on the commerce clause was invalidated by the
Supreme Court. Since then, however, a newly conservative
Supreme Court has begun again to restrain the power of the
federal government, and this judicial activism is jeopardizing
much of our most important social legislation. The Court has
already weakened firearms regulation in schools and protections for women victimized by violence.

Rulings that weaken the Americans with Disabilities Act are
among the closest to my own concerns. Every time I walk past
a building with a ramp in front of it for those in wheelchairs, I
am proud to be an American. In a case two years ago that may
well become historic, the law's requirement to make courts accessible to those in wheelchairs was challenged. The Supreme
Court ruled that court officials could be fined for failing to
meet this requirement. But the case was decided by a slim mar-
gin of five to four, and Justice Sandra Day O'Connor cast the
deciding vote. The question now is whether President Bush's
new appointees to the Court will truly practice judicial restraint
and respect the rule of law established over the past half century, or will seek to write new law, undermining the role of
Congress and reversing the march of progress the nation is
rightly proud of.

The guiding philosophy of the Supreme Court is of great
importance to every person in America, because the decisions
of the Court will affect their lives in countless ways in coming
years, such as whether employees have a right to be protected in
the workplace, whether people have a right to be free from discrimination in all its ugly forms in their daily lives, or whether

environmental laws that keep our air and water clean are valid.

These issues and many others have been addressed by the Supreme Court in recent years. In many of those cases the Court was narrowly divided, and each of these areas is likely to be the subject of additional decisions in the years to come.

The Supreme Court's major role in our national life is not new. When Alexis de Tocqueville described America in the early years of the nineteenth century, he noted that "scarcely any political question arises in the United States that is not resolved, sooner or later, into a judicial question." We are a nation of laws. That is why it is so important for the president to nominate men and women to the bench who are truly independent and who respect the Constitution—not ideological extremists who seek to impose their personal philosophy on the American people. That is why we must all remain vigilant about future nominees to our courts.

Privacy in America

Perhaps the principle we cherish most in this country is our right to privacy. One of the major reasons we fought the revolution was to restrain a tyrannical king from imposing himself on decisions we believe are personal ones. Our choice of religion is a private decision. Who we marry is a private decision. Who we choose as our friends is a private decision. Whether or when we have children is a private decision. The list goes on and on, and modern technology is constantly creating new ways to invade our privacy.

Supreme Court decisions guaranteeing individual privacy are based on the Constitution's protections. But more important, these rights and decisions belong to us because we did not cede them to the government when we adopted the Constitution.

This bedrock principle of privacy, repeatedly upheld by the Supreme Court in numerous decisions over the past half century, is now threatened by the changing composition of the Supreme Court. Clearly, Congress must be willing to subject the president's judicial nominees to close scrutiny and careful questioning, and the president must be willing to provide the information necessary for Congress to make informed decisions.

In the end, voters must elect representatives who will protect their most important interests and recognize how easily power, even in America, can be abused if we do not abide by the Constitution. Three branches checking and balancing one another is the cornerstone of our democracy. If we want to keep it strong, we will.

CHAPTER TWO

Protecting Our National Security

When a bomb failed to go off in Amman, Jordan, in November 2005, it meant a suicide bomber had not completed her murderous mission. But her three companions did, and scores of innocent people, many celebrating a wedding, were killed in three hotels when her fellow terrorists detonated explosions within minutes of one another. The surviving terrorist said she undertook the mission to avenge her brother, a known Al Qaeda terrorist who had been killed in the war in Iraq. She and her terrorist companions chose to attack civilians in Amman because they viewed Jordan as sympathetic to America in the war.

Nothing can justify or explain such wanton murder. Nothing can relieve our deep remorse over lives lost so needlessly.

America suffered its own tragedy of terrorism that fateful day in September 2001. Nearly three thousand innocents were killed. September 11 taught us that we are vulnerable, not invincible. We learned in that instant that we were no longer immune from the festering hatred of peoples ten thousand miles away. September 11 marked one of the most violent of all terrorist acts in a world where terror is now common.

With such new and deadly enemies able to reach our shores,

we needed a new definition of national security. Just as we had to create a new and more enlightened foreign policy to deal with the changed world after World War II, so we now require a new and forward-looking foreign policy for a world that is dangerous in new ways.

But our leaders did not rise to the challenge. Instead, the military aspects of the War on Terror became the single-minded focus of our foreign policy. Terrorism is our greatest threat, and the military aspects are important, but our long-term security and progress also depend heavily on a peaceful world, on progress for all people, on world economic development and the reduction of world poverty, on control of dangerous weapons, and on many other goals. We must deal with complex fundamental problems, such as weak nations that breed terrorism, disease, and pollution. There are problems of poor governance. The array of issues is much broader than can possibly be stated in the bumper-sticker slogan "War on Terror." Nevertheless, we allowed military force to dominate our strategy after September 11 and ignored the wide range of other responses essential for undermining terrorism and achieving our broader security goals.

Rather than looking forward and developing a new concept of national security, we reverted defensively and fearfully to policies of earlier times. Rather than broadening our view of what motivates our enemies and how the battlefield has changed, we narrowed our actions and lost opportunities to wage the battle effectively. Rather than viewing international institutions as effective means to advance our interests, we viewed them as a nuisance. Rather than building and strengthening international alliances to advance our interests, we charted a unilateral course. Rather than proudly protecting the civil liberties guaranteed by our Constitution as a message of hope and freedom to our enemies, we undermined our own basic liberties. We refused to heed past lessons of success and failure, and we did not make America safer.

After 9/11 we had the sympathy and concern of the world. People everywhere responded by saying that they are all Americans. Other nations recognized the value of America's leadership and wanted our credibility to be strong. They understood that their own greatest guarantee of long-term peace and stability is for the United States to live up to its ideals as a beacon to the rest of the world. We had long been honored for our democratic values and admired for our economic achievements. But we squandered this reservoir of admiration and moral authority. Our misguided policies reduced rather than enhanced our influence in the world, created new battalions of terrorists, and made it far more difficult to protect our nation and its interests.

The war in Iraq, as many had warned, turned Iraq into a breeding ground of terrorism, which it had not been before. It inflamed anti-American passions in much of the Middle East and elsewhere in the world. Going to war was the wrong way to stop terrorism, and it was the wrong way to make America safe.

I am always astonished when some say it does not matter that so many in the world no longer respect America. Of course it matters. Respect is the most important source of our influence. Respect for our ideals and way of life is a powerful incentive to peace and democracy everywhere. It enables us to negotiate from strength. We are trusted by our friends, and we can mobilize our allies to pressure our opponents. Sadly, many Iraqis have come to see us as occupiers, not liberators. The "cakewalk" mentality that launched the war and botched the peace was a disaster.

Of especially large concern is the new policy of "preventive" war that defies our historical traditions. The Bush administration's concept of such warfare and the arrogant way it has been applied have made the world more dangerous, not less dangerous, for our people. Our subsequent loss of moral authority has been exacerbated by our flagrant and irresponsible use of torture and our cynical disdain for the widely respected Geneva Conventions.

Our moral authority was also needlessly diminished when we took steps to reduce our commitment to the basic rights of our people here at home. The Patriot Act was used by the administration to condone far-reaching searches that are a clear abrogation of our basic rights. The act, adopted in the immediate aftermath of 9/11, was meant to be temporary, but the Bush administration and the Republican Congress have been eager to extend its abusive provisions.

The world has stopped listening to us the way it once did. We have strained close alliances that were indispensable in advancing our interests so well for so long, and doing so has undermined our credibility and influence. What gives our foreign policy credibility and strength and makes the nation more secure is our adherence to the basic principles and protections written into our Constitution. Our moral authority is a vital source of our national security. We cannot expect the world to do as we say if what we do defies our ideals and antagonizes other people in other lands.

We can make America safe again from terrorists and other potential enemies. We can diminish the threats of nuclear war and terrorism. We can reduce violence around the world. We can heal the festering wounds of poverty and national humiliation. But to do so, we must have a policy that is forthright, honest, and attuned to the changing world and the rise of powerful new economies in other lands. We need a foreign policy based on multilateralism, not unilateralism. As the Declaration of Independence states, we owe a "decent respect to the opinions of mankind." We need a foreign policy grounded in courage and patience, not in fear and vengeance.

A New Definition of National Security

Important lessons can be gained from our successful foreign policy after World War II. The Soviet Union had become a superpower that was antagonistic toward America and our allies in Western Europe. The nuclear age had begun. We had developed the atomic bomb in the desert of New Mexico and had used it to end World War II, but more than half a century since then, no nuclear weapon has been exploded in anger anywhere on earth.

But the development and proliferation of such weapons has exploded. In 1952, we tested a hydrogen bomb seven hundred times more powerful than our first atomic bombs. The following year the Soviet Union announced that it, too, had such a weapon. Soon, England and France had nuclear weapons as well. In 1964, China tested its own nuclear bomb. A world war with nuclear weapons could end life on earth. Tens of millions died in the last century's two world wars. Europe lost 36 million people, the Soviet Union 50 million. But now the stakes are dramatically higher.

We developed a new definition of national security for that time. We also developed a new foreign policy, with military, diplomatic, and economic components. We invested in our military capabilities. We adopted a policy of containment of the Soviet Union rather than outright invasion. We spent prodigiously on the reconstruction of the countries of our former enemies in World War II and they have become leading democracies and allies today.

The world has changed as radically in recent years as it did in the aftermath of World War II. Today, our newest enemies are extremist terrorists who belong to no nation and who wander the world to spread violence. They are driven by complex factors, including poverty, religious fanaticism, frustration, and alienation. None of this justifies what they do. But they have the potential to arm themselves with weapons of mass destruction, possibly using rogue nuclear material from the former Soviet Union or new chemical or biological agents.

Our national security policies must make us safe not only from the arsenals of other nations but from the unsecured nuclear weapons materials available to belligerent groups anywhere in the world. Nuclear nonproliferation must continue to be our highest priority.

Dealing with these threats is essential, but they are not our only national security concerns. Efforts toward nuclear disarmament have faltered. Some sovereign nations, notably North Korea and Iran, are obvious nuclear threats. North Korea already has such weapons, and Iran seems bent on acquiring them. There are bitter boundary disputes between Pakistan and India, and both nations have these weapons. Other nations are growing wealthy and powerful and are likely to develop advanced military capabilities. The balance of power in the coming generation will shift, and we must plan for this now.

Another important national security concern is our thirst for oil, which has made us heavily dependent on the oil reserves of Arab countries and other foreign nations. Any foreign policy adequate to these times must include an effective energy policy that frees us from dependency on nations with different values and antagonistic interests.

Among the most subtle sources of international power are the trade in goods and services and the flow of capital. Short-sighted economic policies have made us dependent both on cheap foreign goods to satisfy consumers and on our ability to borrow from other nations to compensate for our mushrooming national debt, which is exacerbated each year by huge deficits in the federal budget. Nations such as China lend us tens of billions of dollars a year. We cannot allow our foreign policy to be dependent on nations that lend us money. This issue, too, must be a priority in our modern world.

Our new definition of national security can no longer be limited to protecting our nation from attack by the military weapons of the past. Our national security planning must now encompass our highways and subways, our dams and electrical facilities, our waste plants and water supplies, our chemical plants and nuclear power plants, and our ability to deal with dangerous epidemics. Homeland security is a new and urgent and complex undertaking.

Our national security also requires scrupulous protection of our democratic ideals so that our example can be a model for the world. When Americans themselves insist on these values, we are a stronger nation and our ideals are more likely to take root elsewhere as well. Democracy cannot be imposed through the barrels of our guns. It must arise from the wishes of a country's own citizens. We know how to persuade by example. We have done so time and again in Latin America, Asia, South America, Eastern Europe, the nations of the former Soviet Union, and in other parts of the world. Surely we can do it now as well.

The Tragedy of Preventive War

We have had many extraordinary successes in the past fifty years. Few people in 1945 believed another world war was preventable but for decades, our policy of containment was successful against our principal rival, the Soviet Union. We contributed through the Marshall Plan and other programs to the astonishing recovery and redevelopment of Germany and Japan, making new allies of former bitter enemies. We limited the spread of nuclear weapons. We encouraged the growth of democracy around the world. We developed a stable international financial system and expanded world trade dramatically.

These accomplishments were neither accidents of history

nor inevitable. When we succeeded, as with the Soviet Union, we did so because we knew who our enemy was and when military intervention should and should not be used. When we failed, as with the war in Vietnam, we understood neither of these factors.

The question of whether our nation should have attacked Iraq is now part of that ongoing all-important debate about how, when, and where our country should use its unsurpassed military might in the years ahead.

In 2002, the Bush administration unveiled its new "National Security Strategy," in which they purported to address the new realities of our age, particularly the proliferation of weapons of mass destruction and terrorist networks with fanatical agendas. They claimed that these new threats were so novel and dangerous that we should "not hesitate to act alone, if necessary, to exercise our right of self-defense by acting pre-emptively."

The administration's discussion of self-defense used the terms "preemptive war" and "preventive war" interchangeably. In international relations, however, these two terms have very different meanings. Traditionally, preemptive action refers to moments when nations react to an imminent threat of attack. When Egyptian and Syrian forces mobilized on Israel's borders in 1967, the threat was obvious and immediate, and Israel was justified in launching a preemptive attack. The global community is tolerant of such actions. No nation should have to suffer a certain first strike before it has the right to act.

In contrast, preventive military action refers to military strikes against a country before it has developed a capability that could someday become a threat. Preventive attacks generally have been condemned. A notorious example was the sneak attack on Pearl Harbor in 1941, a preventive strike by Japan to block a planned military buildup by the United States in the Pacific. The premeditated nature of preventive attacks and preventive wars makes them anathema to well-established international principles against aggression.

Historically, the United States has condemned the idea of preventive war, arguing correctly that it violates these basic international principles. But at times in our history, preventive war has been seriously advocated as a policy option.

During the initial years of the Cold War some of our military and civilian experts advocated a preventive war against the Soviet Union. They proposed a first strike that would devastate the nation and prevent it from developing a nuclear capability threatening to our security. At the time they claimed that the uniquely destructive power of nuclear weapons required us to ignore traditional international rules, much as the Bush administration's national security strategy attempts to justify preventive war to deal with new threats in today's world. But as President Harry Truman once stated, "You don't 'prevent' anything by war . . . except peace."

Instead of launching a surprise first strike in the Cold War, our nation dedicated itself, after much internal and often bitter debate, to a strategy of deterrence and containment that successfully kept the peace during long and frequently difficult years that included dangerous confrontations across the globe.

The argument that the United States should take military action, even in the absence of an imminent attack, did not disappear, however. Arguments for preventive war resurfaced again in the Eisenhower administration in 1953, but President Eisenhower and Secretary of State John Foster Dulles decided firmly against it. President Eisenhower emphasized that even if we were to win such a war we would face vast burdens of occupation and reconstruction that would come afterward.

The argument arose again in 1962, when President Kennedy learned that the Soviet Union would soon have the ability to launch nuclear missiles from Cuba against our country. Many military officers urged the president to approve a preventive attack to destroy this capability before it became operational. Robert Kennedy, however, like Harry Truman, argued that such a first strike was inconsistent with American values. He said that a surprise first strike against Cuba would be a Pearl Harbor in reverse. "For 175 years," he said, "we have not been that kind of country."

His view prevailed. President Kennedy had learned an important lesson from the disastrous experience of the Bay of Pigs invasion a year earlier—a mistake he admitted—and he was reluctant to use military force. Instead, he blockaded Cuba and demanded the withdrawal of the missiles by a specific deadline. In the fateful showdown that October, the Soviet Union relented. Peace was preserved, and a new basis for agreements on nuclear arms control was created.

As these examples show, American thinkers have long debated the merits of preventive war. No one would deny our right to use military force to prevent an imminent attack on our country, and to do so unilaterally if necessary. But preventive war is consistent with neither our values nor our national security.

The world suddenly changed for America on 9/11, but the

Bush administration's "National Security Strategy" is too extreme. It legitimizes a first strike, and elevates it to a core security doctrine. Disregarding precedents of international law, the strategy asserts, in effect, that our unique military preeminence exempts us from the rules we expect other nations to obey— and the war in Iraq was launched.

War should always be our last resort. Instead, the Bush administration made preventive war an option of first resort. It wrongly used preventive war for regime change in Iraq, and it did so essentially unilaterally. If there was a legitimate justification for war, we should have been able to persuade the international community to join us in large numbers. There was no reason to go to war when we did. United Nations inspectors were in Iraq searching for the weapons of mass destruction that we now know did not exist.

Might cannot make America right. We cannot write our own rules for the modern world. To do so deprives our great nation of the moral legitimacy so necessary to promote our values abroad. It gives other nations an excuse to violate fundamental principles of civilized international behavior, and the downward spiral we initiate could well engulf the whole planet.

Lessons from the Past

Lessons from our past are also being ignored today. Our first responsibility is to be certain we have the military capability to protect American citizens and keep our country safe. But we have learned that an intelligent foreign policy requires the help of our friends. We successfully contained the Soviet Union with the concerted support of our allies in Europe, Asia, Africa, and Latin America. We must take unilateral action if required when our security depends on it, but whenever we can, we should work with others for our national security .

During the long Cold War confrontation with the Soviet Union, our friends allowed us to use their countries for our bases, and they supported nuclear nonproliferation. Many helped spread democracy through example, condemning Soviet expansionism and providing aid to developing and poor nations. We cannot deal well with our enemies unless we deal constructively in full and respectful partnerships with our friends. This principle applies in particular to rising powers such as China and India. We must include them in our planning, and bring our differences to the negotiating table. As always, we must negotiate from strength, but we must also recognize the views and fears of our adversaries and the potential grounds for agreement and friendship.

We have also learned that our democratic values can be promoted most effectively when we abide by them ourselves. We did not always do so, and we paid a price. The misleading claims about the war in Vietnam, the Watergate break-in, the Cambodian bombings, the secretive and illegal Iran-contra arrangements, and other regrettable decisions aroused suspicion of our true motives around the world.

But our moral commitment to nuclear disarmament, our overall respect for other nations, our democratic values, and our valiant commitment during the two world wars still made us the most admired nation in the world. The earth is a far more democratic planet than it was half a century ago, in large part because of America's example. Without firing a shot, South Africa abandoned apartheid. Chile, Argentina, and other nations in Latin America became democracies. Many of the former nations of the Soviet Union are now on a path to democracy or have already reached it. Some will perhaps reverse course. But our message of equality and liberty has traveled the world.

A key aspect of our foreign policy is that Americans must remain confident and proud of the values of their nation. Jefferson asserted this principle when he was president. In the face of what America perceived as potential threats from more powerful nations at the time, including Britain, Spain and France, he was confident that America, despite its youth, would remain independent and become strong because all Americans had a true stake in their country's future.

When we lose confidence in our government and become cynical about our own principles, we risk becoming weak. With confidence, we can deal from strength. When political opportunists play on our fears, America is less likely to be the great nation it has been and should be.

A New Foreign Policy Framework

The war in Iraq and the War on Terror have been fought without a strategy that can lead to true success. Half a century ago we lived in a bipolar world with the United States and our allies in Europe and Japan on one side and the Soviet Union and its satellites on the other. We succeeded because we understood our enemies and how to deal with them. Today our enemies are widely dispersed and harder to pinpoint. Our foreign policy, nevertheless, can be as successful as in the past.

Among our most tragic errors is that we have not clearly defined our new enemy. Saddam Hussein was a tyrant, but he was not the source of the terrorist threat to our nation. The intelligence gathered by the administration alledgedly connecting Saddam Hussein to Al Qaeda was never credible and turned out to be false. Claims about uranium purchases from abroad and Saddam Hussein's imminent ability to acquire nuclear weapons turned out to be bogus.

I fully supported the invasion of Afghanistan to hunt down Osama bin Laden and his henchmen in the aftermath of the attacks on September 11. I fully supported Secretary of State Colin Powell in his successful mission to build a broad coalition of allies to support the Afghan invasion. It was the right start to a successful War on Terror.

But we soon diverted our attention from this battle. Bin Laden escaped and Afghanistan was neglected. The administration rushed to war in Iraq without a broad coalition of support and with no economic and diplomatic plan to win the peace and stabilize the nation after Saddam Hussein was removed from power.

We made a series of important mistakes that can serve as valuable lessons in the development of a new and better framework for our foreign policy.

- We confused who the enemy was. Rather than stay focused on Osama bin Laden, we went to war against Saddam Hussein.

- We did not act on the basis of meticulously and objectively gathered evidence, the way President Kennedy did when he faced down the Soviet Union during the Cuban Missile Crisis. Instead, the administration cherry-picked the intelligence it needed to justify immediate war.

- We lost our patience. I strongly support the development of democracy around the world and the spread of human rights, but these goals require years to achieve. We cannot impose democracy overnight through military intervention. Imposing democracy is itself a contradiction in terms. It must come from the bottom up. The task of establishing democracy does not end when the first free and fair elections are held. It's not enough to give people the right to vote. Democracy must deliver jobs, basic services, and a higher quality of life as well.

- We failed to act in a genuinely multilateral way. Even in the clearly bipolar world of the Cold War, America pursued coalitions with other nations to support our foreign policy. Those nations provided us with military, moral, and other support. In going to war in Iraq, we strained our alliances and our standing in the international community. As a result, we largely bore the military responsibility for the war ourselves, and sowed distrust among those who had doubts about our motives and the need for war.

■ The invasion had widespread ramifications that were not considered. Most important, rising anger in the Middle East has made Iraq a hotbed of terrorism it had never been before. It increased anti-American sentiment and made the War on Terror harder to win. Our actions in Iraq may also have had the consequence of accelerating the nuclear development programs of Iran and North Korea. Iran now wields considerable power in Iraq. The great irony is that America went to war in Iraq to remove an Iraqi leader thought to have weapons of mass destruction, but our action may well have made it easier for Iran's leaders to acquire their own weapons of mass destruction.

■ The commitment of our military is open-ended. No realistic criteria have been developed to enable Americans to know when victory is achieved, or even what victory is.

We must not make such profound mistakes again. In considering war and other foreign policy actions we must understand our enemy, gather the best intelligence we can, work with our allies, understand the limits of military might in nation building, and prepare for the inevitable contingencies in this complex world of nations and ethnic groups. We must have effective plans to stabilize and rebuild nations after conflicts. We must recognize that our military will be called on not only to

61

fight well but to participate in the recovery and reconstruction as well. This is the new world in which we live, and it creates new demands on our soldiers, the Pentagon, and the State Department.

In maintaining our national security, however, since prevention of war is more important than military intervention, our foreign policy must include additional components such as forthright and realistic diplomacy, substantial economic aid, financially responsible policies, and sincere and sustained efforts to facilitate the growth of democracy and respect for human rights.

America has played a highly constructive role so far in facilitating the resolution of the Israeli-Palestinian conflict. Israelis have the undeniable right to live within safe and secure borders, free from the daily threat of terrorism. At the same time, the Palestinians have aspirations that must be addressed. America cannot impose a solution, but our nation and our leadership and our active participation can make an indispensable contribution to the achievement of a lasting peace. We must be tireless in supporting those who seek genuine peace in the Middle East, wherever they come from. It's the right thing to do, and it's the best way to reduce terrorism.

Having the finest military in the world is a vital part of our foreign policy. Nations will understand the force we can deploy if force is necessary. But a core principle of our foreign policy is that America must abide by the rules we set for others. We cannot ask others to reduce or forgo nuclear arsenals when we expand our own. We cannot demand democracy for others if we fail to live scrupulously by our own Constitution. We must, in fact, be the world's great example of decency, democracy, and human rights. It is the only realistic way to influence the world's rising powers as well as our antagonists in the Middle East. With the right policies, we can both protect ourselves and win new friends to the cause of democracy.

Winning

One of the reasons we enjoy sports so much is that, when the final whistle blows, there is a winner and a loser. Progress in world affairs is more difficult to measure. I am always disturbed that Democrats are sometimes thought to be weak on national defense, when in fact we are the ones who have dealt most forthrightly and realistically with the complexities of our changing world. We combine a complex view of the world with clear support for national strength.

Woodrow Wilson and Franklin Delano Roosevelt led the nation to victory in two world wars. Harry Truman faced up to the awesome responsibility of nuclear power and had the courage to restrain its use when the Cold War began. President Kennedy stared down the Soviet Union in the world's most dangerous nuclear confrontation to date. In all these cases, America emerged the victor, strong and safe.

We must apply that framework to the battle against terrorism. To do so, we must first understand who the terrorists are. They typically do not owe allegiance to any sovereign nation. They may house themselves temporarily in nations such as Afghanistan and now Iraq. But the battlefield is always changing. It can move from New York to Baghdad to Madrid to London to Amman. It is a war they fight by stealth, with no respect for civilian life.

Because terrorists travel from country to country, we need the cooperation and good faith of as many nations as possible. We need good intelligence, good law enforcement, and effective diplomatic cooperation to ferret out terrorist cells that are active in Europe, the Middle East, Asia, and other regions.

Fighting terrorism requires ongoing and expanded investments in human intelligence as well. We spend billions of dollars each year on intelligence, and we have technologies of incredible sophistication. But we lack adequate numbers of trained agents on the ground to locate cells and track key leaders. Our knowledge of Arabic and other critical languages is insufficient to meet the challenge. Since money is a lifeline for terrorist organizations, international cooperation is essential to enable us to choke off this financing.

Terrorists have many and complex motives. Often, they are well-educated, middle- and upper-class individuals, and they obtain their support from weak and dangerous governments. A foreign policy designed to defeat terrorism must acknowledge that supporting economic development is a necessity. It must also deal with the alienated Muslim communities in Western Europe that find an identity and an alternative leader in Osama bin Laden.

Winning the hearts and minds of the Muslim world is essential. Support for terrorism is not unshakeable in that world. The brutality and indiscriminate attacks by terrorists in nations such as Indonesia, Morocco, and Turkey will isolate the extremists and strengthen the moderates in those countries. Positive American policies make a very real difference. When we abused prisoners in Iraq, our standing plunged. But when we provided assistance to Muslim nations, as we did after the devastating tsunami in South Asia and the earthquake in Pakistan, our standing increased.

Homeland Security

Homeland security is the domestic aspect of the War on Terror. The extensive damage done by Hurricane Katrina is a clear reminder that a nation as developed, wealthy, and interconnected as ours is especially vulnerable to a well-placed bomb. When the levees gave way in New Orleans, the damage was unimaginable. The tragically slow reaction of the Federal Emergency Management Agency, the agency established to manage such disasters, demonstrates that the Bush administration has failed to take homeland security seriously. The president's plan to protect the nation against a potential epidemic of avian flu could easily become a classic case of too little too late. His own appointees concede it will take years to be prepared.

Early last year, President Bush's deputy secretary for Homeland Security, Admiral James Loy, told the Senate Intelligence Committee, "We believe that attacking the homeland remains at the top of al-Qaeda's operation priority list . . ." He went on, "Thus, the probability of an attack in the United States is assessed to be high . . ."

Nevertheless, the homeland security effort remains dangerously disorganized. Functions are dispersed that must be centralized. Information is not adequately shared. Lines of authority and coordination are unclear. FEMA's failure is an example we had better heed.

A principal concern is securing our borders. We should work with Canada and Mexico to develop a North America–wide immigration policy to protect our borders from potential terrorists. We cannot secure our borders on our own; our northern and southern borders are too porous and too difficult to monitor.

Biometric technology can be used more effectively. Remarkable progress has been made in developing such technology, which can identify persons through their finger veins, eyes, and other biological traits, but we are not yet using these technologies adequately.

We must be careful, however, not to undermine civil liberties and screen out innocent people. I have been stopped trying to board a plane because my name, not an uncommon one, was on a watch list. We must also be sensitive to the fact that long lines at borders can undermine commerce. Nevertheless, much more can be done with advanced technology, and we can use existing technology to carry out much more of the detailed work required. We also need a far bolder strategy to combat the health risks of biological and chemical attacks.

Nuclear Nonproliferation

Terrorism is our newest enemy, but the spread of nuclear weapons remains our greatest threat. On this issue, the Bush administration has been dangerously irresponsible. It has come perilously close to launching a new nuclear arms race.

The progress made in the post–World War II years to limit and control nuclear weapons is among our greatest foreign policy successes. Yet the Bush administration has turned its back on this progress. The Nuclear Non-Proliferation Treaty was the foundation of these efforts. President Johnson signed it, President Nixon saw it through Congress, and nearly two hundred nations have voluntarily forgone nuclear weapons because of it. Presidents Ford, Carter, and Reagan, along with the first President Bush and President Clinton, all championed nuclear arms reduction treaties, which have substantially cut back the nuclear arsenals of both the United States and the former Soviet Union.

The Bush administration, however, has moved in the opposite direction. It has initiated research into new kinds of nuclear weapons, known as "mininukes" and "bunker busters," for battlefield use and the destruction of underground bunkers. How can the administration ask other nations, such as North Korea and Iran, to forgo nuclear weapons, and then develop new types of such weapons for us to use?

Mohamed ElBaradei, the director of the International Atomic Energy Agency and winner of the Nobel Peace Prize in 2005, put it this way: "There are some who have continued to dangle a cigarette from their mouth and tell everybody else not to smoke." Blatant hypocrisy is a nonstarter in foreign policy. To have a serious nonproliferation effort, we should cancel the mininuke and bunker buster programs and revitalize our nuclear arms control and reduction efforts. We must also take immediate, stronger steps to protect the loosely guarded sites where nuclear materials, and even nuclear weapons, may be accessible to terrorists, and adopt strict international controls over the export of nuclear materials. In addition, we should mount an urgent effort to develop new technologies capable of detecting nuclear materials that smugglers may attempt to bring across borders.

At the heart of our efforts to reduce the spread of nuclear weapons is the need for serious cooperation from our allies around the world. Our unilateral policies have undermined their trust in us, and the challenge is now far more difficult that it ought to be.

The Damage Done

National security cannot be single-minded. The almost obsessive focus of the Bush administration on Saddam Hussein and the war in Iraq has caused widespread damage. We have neglected our own military, which has been stretched to the breaking point. Our ability to attract recruits has been severely damaged.

An administration that is spending $5 billion each month on the war in Iraq cannot easily finance a stronger military.

Our ties with our European allies have been jeopardized by our unilateral actions in Iraq and our insensitivity and abrasiveness on other matters. Pointed rhetorical attacks deriding an "old" and "new" Europe were destructive. Europeans are our closest allies for powerful historical reasons, and cooperation with them is indispensable for effective policies. Without it, success will be difficult to achieve in the battle against terrorists. The support of these allies is essential in intelligence gathering, international finance, and the prosecution of terrorists on their soil. In turn, we must aid them in areas they care strongly about, such as global warming and the development of military technology.

Conclusion

The commitment of our military forces in Iraq cannot be openended. It does not serve our interests, or Iraq's interests, either. Iraq must begin to take responsibility for itself.

As we look to the future, we must remember past mistakes. Congress must take greater responsibility for decisions to go to war. The media must maintain its courage and present diverse and unpopular views. We must demand honesty and openness in our leaders. Success in Iraq is essential, but we cannot afford to ignore other urgent and emerging problems around the world.

Inevitably, the legacy of Iraq will be harmful. If America had allowed the UN inspections to continue, war could have been avoided. We were never given a convincing reason by the administration to remove the inspectors and launch the invasion.

To some, ridding Iraq of Saddam Hussein was justification enough for war. But consider the growing influence of Iran, which is a known supporter of terrorism and which may be pursuing nuclear weapons. Consider the consequences of a policy that produces more preventive wars. Consider the growing strength of the terrorist movement. Consider the casualties. Consider America's lost moral authority and lost respect in the world. It is hard to maintain with a straight face that the war was justified.

President Kennedy was especially concerned about India in his all too brief time in the White House. He worried that India, the new democracy, might side with the Soviet Union, not the democracies of the West. He knew that military strength alone would never be decisive in the battle for the hearts and minds of India's people. Our ideals, our way of life, and our prosperity, he believed, were our greatest allies in this struggle, and he was right. The same is true of the struggle in Iraq today.

By emphasizing what is best about America, we can convince the rest of the world that individual rights, peaceful relations, and democracy are of paramount importance. Our goal is simple but profound. As President Kennedy said, we must "build a world of peace where the weak are safe and the strong are just." Such a world is possible if we have the wisdom and the courage to build it.

CHAPTER THREE

Participating in a Shrinking World

N o one is surprised today that products we buy in local department stores may be made in China, Sri Lanka, Argentina, or other far-off nations. When we call on the phone for help to fix our computers or correct our credit card bills, we may well be speaking to someone in India. Our records are often processed in other nations. Our companies often conduct their research abroad. And, of course, U.S. jobs are affected. When products are made in low-wage nations, their competition affects what companies in America pay for similar work. To be competitive, U.S. firms increasingly contract their work abroad, and American jobs are lost.

Few things will affect us more than our shrinking world. But our leaders have responded hardly at all to the extraordinary changes taking place in how we live, work, learn, communicate, and do business. New technologies have contributed to globalization by making it easier to communicate throughout the world. So have other factors, including the competitive abilities of rapidly growing economies in Asia, Eastern Europe, and South America. Even without the newest technologies, these nations are now formidable competitors. They are building their economies into engines of growth based not only on low wages but on well-educated populations, modern infra-structures, strong health care systems, and well-run businesses. The mobility of capital, which can be invested across the globe in an instant, has also helped shrink the world. Globalization is still in its early stages, and its evolution will cause the world to shrink still more over time.

If America does not respond adequately to these changes, we will lose more jobs, and the jobs that replace them will pay still less. We will forfeit our leadership in developing the world's great technologies. If we respond vigorously, however, globalization will be neither the threat nor the cause for fear that so many seem to believe it is. If we invest in our people, our research, and our businesses, we will create opportunities we could never have imagined before.

This is not wishful thinking. The miracle of our capitalist system, aided and supplemented by a fruitful partnership with government, is that we can all benefit. Just as there has always been enough in America to share, there will be enough in the world if we manage it correctly. We will still need to fully pro-tect employees from layoffs and their loss of benefits. But if America responds wisely to these changes, it will generate the revenues needed to support progressive policies.

To compete today we need an inventive, creative economy in which people matter most. We must prepare every man, woman, and child for the new world of intensifying competi-tion and increasingly sophisticated technologies. American workers and managers have to be the best educated and best trained. A lifetime of training will be one of the keys to global competitiveness, as will an environment that motivates people to be at their inventive and creative best. The foundation is education, which begins virtually at birth and ends only with retirement, if then. We can't afford to leave anyone out. An unproductive American is a lost opportunity for all.

Revitalizing investment in our human capital is not a new challenge for America. Throughout our history we have repeatedly had to raise the educational level of the American people to meet the needs of an evolving and growing economy. In the mid-nineteenth century we created free and mandatory public schools for all, well before most other nations did. At the beginning of the twentieth century we rapidly established new public high schools across America to meet the needs of a nation whose economy was ever more demanding and was facing growing competition from other nations. We subsidized college education to meet the needs of new white-collar industries that required new skills.

As we begin this new century, globalization requires us to move beyond what we have already achieved. Children need to begin their education well before they reach kindergarten, and they need to develop social skills as well. The evidence is now overwhelming that early education is essential and that we must raise the quality of traditional education from kindergarten through high school to keep from falling behind the rest of the developed world. The quality of American education in comparison to other nations is inadequate, and it varies widely from one community to another. These gaps have to be closed. In particular, students must be ready for the transition to college. As the costs of higher education rise, no citizen who is qualified should be deprived of a college education due to cost.

73

Our response to globalization cannot stop there. In addition to improving the quality of education from birth to retirement, we must also do the following:

■ We must invest more heavily in engineering, science, math and the life sciences. Our R&D is not sufficient. It seems likely that this new century will be the century of the life sciences, and our leadership in this area must continue. But there is ample evidence that we are not investing adequately in these subjects at a time when major breakthroughs in research are increasingly taking place in other lands.

■ We must recognize that as we all grow and change, the world's appetite for energy could easily overwhelm our resources, resulting in much higher energy prices. The current trajectory of energy consumption, if it continues, could cripple the planet by polluting our air and water and destroying our wildlife. For America and the world to grow, we must restrain our energy use, which would reduce environmental damage, and develop alternate sources of energy.

■ Our tax system should not continue to subsidize the export of U.S. jobs to foreign nations. We should devise better ways of using our tax laws to create jobs in America.

■ Employees should not bear the full burden of globalization and changing technologies. They deserve a stronger safety net when they lose their jobs through no fault of their own. Unemployment insurance should be modernized, expanded, and made more generous for these new times. Overtime pay must be protected so that businesses do not take advantage of workers. Work must be made more flexible so that businesses can fully utilize the services of the nation's workers and so that workers can take time off from their jobs to care for their children, ill family members, or themselves.

■ Our trading partners, whether rich or poor, should adopt laws that protect their workers and assure them a fair share of the benefits of world trade. Greater international rules are needed in these areas. We must be certain that our businesses are operating on a level playing field so that the cost of doing business is not an unfair burden.

■ We must become partners with other nations in creating a global middle class. Such an achievement would help all nations. Strong international markets for goods and services would support worldwide growth and develop new jobs everywhere.

Globalization is not a new phenomenon. In the late 1800s and early 1900s, world trade grew rapidly. Capital flowed into the United States in search of opportunities to invest in our railroads, steel mills, and other new industries. Steamships and the telegraph made the globe seem miraculously small to the people of those times. As the British economist John Maynard Keynes famously described life before World War I, "The inhabitant of London could order by telephone, sipping his morning tea in bed, the various products of the whole earth, in such quantity as he might see fit and reasonably expect their early delivery upon his doorstep." His words resonate anew as we contemplate the wonders of online shopping today.

75

Trade helped America prosper. Its harmful side effects were tempered by a new era of progressive social reforms, including women's suffrage, worker protections, the income tax, and, not least, the direct popular election of senators, which made Congress more responsive to the needs of the nation. Until the adoption of the Seventeenth Amendment to the Constitution in 1913, senators were chosen by the legislature of each state.

The globalization of goods and capital was set back for decades by the two world wars and the Depression in between. But it resumed in the 1950s. New trade agreements increased the flow of goods between Europe and America and Japan. A new and healthy world financial system emerged from international agreements reached at Bretton Woods, New Hampshire, under President Roosevelt in 1944. America's economy grew so rapidly that other nations feared that powerful multinational corporations based in the United States would undermine prosperity elsewhere.

By the 1970s, American multinational corporations were no longer feared. Instead, American businesses began to fear new overseas giants such as Toyota and Sony. Japanese and European companies, spurred on by technological and managerial innovations, made deep inroads into American markets as we began to import a far greater portion of the goods and services we consumed.

Pessimists believed American industry could not be revived, but by the 1990s American technological companies such as Microsoft, Intel, and Cisco dominated world markets. Today, more and more products are a mouse click away. With a laptop, we can work anywhere and shop anywhere, and companies can produce, if not anywhere, in more and more places. The Internet has transformed communications. Cell phones can reach everywhere, take our pictures, play our favorite television programs, and bring vast amounts of information to our fingertips.

America has taken the lead in many of these areas. But other nations are now becoming formidable competitors, and not due solely to technology. A software designer working in Bangalore, India, can do so not only because of the Internet, but also because of India's growing economy and a good education. Manufacturers in China make first-rate goods—not only because of new technologies, but also because of capital investments and an educated and increasingly well trained labor force.

Fear has accompanied every new stage of globalization, and some inevitably lose out. But for the most part, if government has done its job properly, opportunity has increased, and so has our productivity and our standard of living. But that result is not inevitable. Nations must invest in themselves, and in recent years America has failed to do so. We must respond by welcoming global opportunities, not withdrawing from them, and to do so requires a vigorous commitment to the future.

The Vital Importance of Education

In dealing with this problem, a high priority should be to revitalize education. With better-educated workers, we will get the productive and inventive economy we need in order to compete effectively in this new age. Only with a revitalized education system can we guarantee equal opportunity for all Americans. Our faith in individualism depends heavily on giving all our citizens the means to achieve their full potential. I have no doubt that if our youth are given such opportunities, they will rise to the challenge and we will be a stronger nation in the years ahead.

We've been painfully slow to recognize this challenge. For a quarter century, the gap between what college graduates and high school graduates earn has grown, reflecting the greater need for additional skills in the modern economy. A high school diploma is no longer adequate in the search for a middle-class life. The average college graduate earned $49,000 in 2003; those with a high school diploma earned only $31,000. Those with a master's degree earned, on average, $10,000 a year more than those with a bachelor degree.

Averages can be deceiving, of course. A college degree does not guarantee a good salary, because factors besides education affect job prospects. Children born to parents who went to college also tend to go to college. They have a wider network of job contacts, are familiar with the cultural knowledge of better-off Americans, and have more stable emotional lives. For generations, colleges have served that cultural and networking mission as well as an educational one.

But as college has changed from a benefit for the privileged to the only reliable path to a middle-class life, young people are increasingly aware that four years of college are essential and that a master's degree may be important as well.

The benefits to society are clear: better-trained and better-educated men and women will improve the productivity of our economy and enable us to compete more effectively in the global economy. Well-trained workers help all of us, because the nation's overall productivity rises. Every additional dollar spent on education will pay us back several times over. It will also save on the costs of social programs by reducing or ending disparities such as the following:

- The unemployment rate of white Americans with a college degree was 2.8 percent in 2003, compared to 4.8 percent for those with only a high school diploma.

- The unemployment rate of black Americans with college degrees was 4.5 percent, compared to 9.3 percent for those with only a high school diploma.

- The poverty rate of those with a college degree was about one third of those with only a high school diploma.

- Incarceration rates of college graduates are much lower. Only 0.1 percent of the population with a college degree or higher was incarcerated in 1997, versus 1.2 percent of those with a high school diploma and 1.9 percent of those who didn't complete high school.

As a result, college graduates cost our society much less in terms of government spending for unemployment insurance, welfare and food-stamps, public health care, and law enforcement. Researchers at the RAND Institute estimate that such government savings range from $800 to $2,500 per college graduate annually. Such graduates pay about twice as much in taxes over their lifetime than those with a high school diploma. Every economist agrees that the nation's competitive advantage in the future will depend even more heavily on the quality of its human capital than in the past.

At least partly as a result of substantial increases in federal aid to education, the rate of college attendance increased significantly in recent decades. But the rate has flattened out since the mid-1990s, and it is still too low.

About 40 percent of white Americans between the ages of eighteen and twenty-four attend college, compared to 30 percent of black Americans and 20 percent of Hispanic Americans. This gap between white and minority college attendance must be closed and overall college attendance must be raised.

The rest of the world is catching up with us. We once prided ourselves on having the highest college attendance rate among advanced nations. But in the past decade the proportion of the young who go to college and obtain a degree has risen more rapidly in other countries than in the United States.

An especially serious problem is that we have fallen far behind in the proportion of students who graduate from college with degrees in science, math, computer technology, and engineering. In China, as Figure 1 (opposite) shows, nearly 50 percent of all degrees awarded are in these fields, compared to only 15 percent in the United States. Europe, India, and Japan significantly exceed us as well in those degrees.

Our future growth and even our way of life are increasingly jeopardized by this shortage of American graduates in science, math, and engineering compared to foreign nations. Nearly half of all patents in America are now granted to foreigners. A large proportion of the students in our science and engineering graduate schools are citizens of other nations. Nine out of ten papers accepted for publication by American scientific journals are now authored by foreign researchers, not Americans.

One reason so few talented American students are interested in science, engineering, and math is that careers in fields such as law and business pay more. A typical pharmaceutical company pays its MBAs more than its PhDs in chemistry, and this discrepancy is common throughout American business. We obviously need to provide more aid for college students majoring in math, science, and engineering. To encourage the pursuit of advanced degrees in these subjects, we should make tuition free for needy students in postgraduate programs. We should also find effective ways to include these subjects in the earliest years of education. We cannot afford to concede these key areas of knowledge and expertise to other nations in the years ahead.

We cannot maintain our leadership in technology and the

COUNTRY	PERCENTAGE
China	49.9
France	30.7
Germany	30.8
India	23.5
Japan	22.8
Spain	22.7
U.K.	25.0
European Union	26.6
U.S.	15.4

SOURCE: NATIONAL SCIENCE FOUNDATION

Figure 1. **Percentage of All Bachelor Degrees Awarded in 2000 in Science, Math, Computer Technology, and Engineering**

global economy unless we produce the minds that can lead the way. By failing to do so, we are ceding our preeminence in these fields to other nations.

How can we do better in educating our people? We know that income matters in determining who goes to college. The proportion of those who go to college is 26 percent greater among families whose incomes are in the highest quarter than in the lowest, so raising parents' wages is a relevant issue. Lower-income students are also more likely to go to two-year colleges and their job prospects are not as good as those who graduate from four-year colleges. A realistic plan to meet this challenge begins at the beginning.

Revolutionizing Early Childhood Education

Years ago, the Senate launched a mentoring program in which senators themselves participate. Every week I meet for an hour with a first-grade student and we take turns reading aloud. I have formed close bonds with several of these children over the years, and I have seen through direct experience the difference that personal attention and caring can make in educational achievement.

My own family experience taught me this basic principle. My mother was the greatest teacher I ever had. She would ask us to diagram a sentence, translate a line of Latin, or recite the names of all the presidents. No one was quicker at it than she. She forced our young minds to work, and she instilled a life-long thirst for knowledge.

Even those who go to public school and go on to college are

not being adequately prepared. We know we must begin to invest more in the very young. As David Hamburg of the Carnegie Corporation has said, "Education does not begin with kindergarten. It begins with prenatal care." Educational investment today must be on a continuum that begins before birth and lasts a lifetime.

The evidence is overwhelming that money spent well on young children will improve their learning skills. It will also improve their social skills, which are very important for doing well in school. We already spend billions of dollars a year on pre-school education, but most of these programs are inadequate. They serve too few children and their quality is often poor. According to one survey, one out of four kindergarten students does not have grade-level emotional, motor, or social skills. Only half of lower-income kindergarten children can recognize letters of the alphabet, compared to two thirds of all kindergarten students. Researchers believe that the lack of preparation for preschool accounts for half of the difference in achievement between black and white students later in their schooling.

Middle-income and lower-income children have less access to good programs to prepare them for kindergarten. A widespread program for children before they reach kindergarten age will help equalize opportunity. Less than half of all children entering kindergarten have attended such a program, but two thirds of those from affluent families have done so.

One highly successful effort for poor children, the Perry Pre-School Program headquartered in Michigan, began more than thirty years ago and its results have been extraordinary.

Both learning and social skills measurably improved among children in the program.

Studies of other programs, including the federal Head Start program launched in 1965, reinforce these findings. Children from such programs have significant benefits that are measurable well into adulthood. They require fewer special education programs, thus reducing costs for public schools, and are more likely to go to college. Their earnings are higher over time, and they pay more taxes. They are healthier, less likely to smoke, and less likely to be on welfare as adults.

We all benefit from such programs, especially parents who are able to work because of them. Between 1970 and 2003, the percentage of women in the labor force increased from 43 percent to 60 percent, and the percentage of married women who were working and had children under six doubled from 30 percent to 60 percent.

America should establish a nationwide program for children under five years old that covers everyone, rich and poor, and of all ethnic and racial backgrounds. The cost may be high, but the returns to society will be far higher. A reasonable estimate is that the benefit to society may be as high as seven times the investment in these young minds. The question is not whether we can afford such a program but whether we can afford to let such a unique opportunity pass.

Improving Elementary and Secondary Schools

Globalization has also highlighted the inadequacy and inequality of traditional public education. From kindergarten through twelfth grade, our schools are not keeping up with their counterparts abroad.

According to an international assessment of the reading and math skills of fifteen-year-olds, the United States ranked 24th among 29 industrial and developing nations. In a study of fourth graders, we ranked 20th out of 25 nations. In math, our eighth graders ranked 20th out of 45 nations. A Gallup poll in the summer of 2005 found that more than half of U.S. parents were either "completely dissatisfied" or "somewhat dissatisfied" with their children's schooling.

Achievement and the quality of education are highly unequal in our country. Reading proficiency differs widely by state, reflecting major differences in standards, teacher quality, and financing. Participation of students in preschool and special education programs is often low in states with the worst performance records and the fewest after-school activities. In some states, the proportion of students who are proficient in reading is only half that in other states. The quality of state tests is highly uneven, and they are poor indicators of performance.

Many states are trying to rig the system. Based on state tests, 70 to 80 percent of students are considered proficient in many states. But national tests show that the proficiency level in some of those states is only 20 or 30 percent.

Local communities vary widely. In Connecticut, Massachusetts, and New York student achievement is excellent in some communities, but in others, especially in inner cities, achievement is as poor as anywhere else in the nation.

Where children go to school is a major factor in their chance for success, and that decision is often based on family income. Only 15 percent of fourth graders in low-income families attain proficiency in reading, compared to 41 percent of students in families with higher incomes. The divide follows racial lines as well. Thirty-nine percent of white fourth graders read proficiently, compared to 12 percent of black fourth graders and 14 percent of Latinos. Once a gap emerges in elementary school, it usually continues through high school and can last a lifetime.

To compete in today's global economy we cannot accept achievement levels that differ so drastically. Such gaps are not what America means by "equal opportunity." We cannot put children at a disadvantage because they are born in the wrong state, in the wrong city, or to low-income parents. We cannot afford to waste the talent and energy of any child.

Testing is controversial, because tests are expensive and teachers often teach to the tests, but a reasonable amount of reliable testing is the most effective way to monitor student achievement. We must also improve curricula and broaden them to include civics, history, music, and the arts. Children need books and other supplies. Good after-school activities are essential, especially to keep young students off the streets, away from drugs, out of trouble, and involved in worthwhile experiences.

One of the most important improvements is to raise the quality of teachers. We need to encourage good people to enter and stay in teaching. Generous tuition assistance for college students who agree to teach for at least four years after graduation would be a strong incentive. We should reward the best teachers with promotions and higher salaries, and offer higher pay for teachers who serve in troubled schools or have expertise in math, science, and special education.

We must find effective ways to retain good teachers. Too many leave teaching early for a variety of reasons, but low pay is a major factor. Teachers earn on average almost $8,000 less than comparable graduates in other fields, and the gap almost triples to $23,000 after fifteen years. Thirty-seven percent of former teachers say low salaries are the main reason they left the classroom before retirement.

To compete in the world and achieve equality of opportunity throughout the nation, the federal government must have a strong role in elementary and secondary education. I was proud to support President Bush's No Child Left Behind Act, which he signed in 2002 and that promised far-reaching school reform. But one of my greatest disappointments is that he has failed to fund it adequately. It is unrealistic to require high national standards for all students but deny communities the financial support they need to improve student achievement.

The need for more active involvement by the federal government in financing elementary and secondary education is clear. Despite state attempts to equalize funding, too many local communities are dependent on local property taxes to pay for their schools, and the funds collected from those taxes vary widely within each state and from state to state.

The federal government now finances only about 8 percent of elementary and secondary education. Over time, I believe the funding should be shared equally so that the federal, state, and local governments each contribute a third of the cost. Such a step does not mean federal control of local schools. There would still be substantial flexibility at local levels and safeguards to prevent federal intrusions, but the overall quality of education in America would be improved significantly.

Enhancing College Enrollment

Sadly, countless students who qualify for college are unable to attend today because of high tuition and inadequate aid. No qualified American student should be denied the opportunity for college because of its cost.

The College Board estimates that, adjusted for inflation, average tuition and fees at four-year public colleges have increased by an incredible 40 percent over the past five years alone. For two-year public colleges, the increase was 26 percent. For countless students, the cost of college is increasingly out of reach. The federal government provides the largest share of grant and loan aid for higher education. Yet the most important form of this aid, the Pell grant, has plummeted as a share of tuition increases. In the mid-1970s the maximum Pell grant equaled 84 percent of the average cost of attending public colleges; currently it is 36 percent. Other supportive programs, including those administered by states, have also failed to keep up with tuition increases.

As a result, students are forced to take out higher and higher loans for college. In the school year 1999–2000, 64 percent of students had obtained federal loans and graduated with an average federal debt of $17,000. By contrast, in 1992–93, only 42 percent of students had federal loans, and their average debt was $9,000.

California in the early 1990s offers a striking example of the way in which financial need deters college enrollment. When tuition was raised and aid reduced, enrollment fell by two hundred thousand students. Across the country, high school students from low-income families without adequate financial aid are affected the most.

Raising tuition without a corresponding increase in student aid has seriously undermined the promise the nation has been making since the success of the landmark G.I. Bill of Rights half a century ago, which made a college education possible for veterans of World War II. Now, in a globalized economy, it is even more important to keep this promise. I've proposed that every child in America, on reaching eighth grade, be offered a contract. Let students sign it, along with their parents and Uncle Sam. The contract will state that if you work hard, finish high school, and are accepted for college, the federal government will guarantee you the cost of earning a degree. Surely we have reached a stage in America where we can say it and mean it. The benefit to the American economy will be enormous.

We must also prepare high school students more effectively for college and the future. Schools and teachers must improve their understanding of how to shape school curricula to the modern needs of colleges, businesses, and the military, and federal support is essential here as well.

Job Training for Life

Another clear and urgent priority in preparing our citizens to compete in the global economy is more effective job training.

All Americans should have opportunities throughout their careers to learn to master emerging technologies and to navigate the rapid changes taking place in the workforce.

In states across the country, large numbers of men and women are on the unemployment rolls when there are large numbers of jobs available. Nationally, more than 7 million Americans are searching for jobs while employers are searching for men and women able to fill almost 4 million job vacancies.

We can do much to fill these vacancies by providing people with the skills to perform for them. Job training is a realistic way to strengthen our economy and enable American workers to continue to be what they always have been—the best in the world.

Yet job training has been a low priority for the White House and the Labor Department over the past five years, in spite of the troubled job market. During that period federal job-training funds were reduced by hundreds of millions of dollars, denying hundreds of thousands of workers the chance to upgrade their skills and qualify for today's jobs.

Numerous ways are available to assure that such training is relevant to the job market. Partnerships among colleges, industry, and labor are especially effective and can emphasize new research and development so that workers trained in the new technologies will be ready when the technologies reach the marketplace.

Our failure to invest adequately in job training is shortsighted economics, and it shortchanges the dreams of Americans who seek the dignity of hard work and are eager to provide for their families.

I have seen firsthand how job training can offer workers exciting new lives. I visited a program of the carpenters' union in Las Vegas that teaches workers the skills for finishing drywall. Graduates of the school perform the task three times more rapidly than those without the training. They produced a better product for their employers, and they earned more because they have strong skills and are more reliable employees.

I have seen this success repeated over and over, in training programs for high-tech workers conducted by the electrical workers' union and for nurses conducted by the service employees' union. Many employers have similar programs. It makes obvious sense for Congress to encourage such training nationwide.

Conserving Energy and Reducing Our Dependence on Foreign Oil

On the issue of energy use, the United States has a special obligation to the world. With 5 percent of the world's population, we account for 25 percent of its energy consumption, most of which is by automobiles and trucks. As a result, we have higher carbon emissions than any other nation on earth. China, with four times our population, only uses one third as much energy.

The need to reduce our demand for energy and develop alternatives to the use of oil is of vital concern to the environment, the economy, and our national security. The danger of global warming is such a serious threat to the entire planet that our refusal to recognize it and act against it is beyond belief. The disruption of oil supplies after Hurricane Katrina was a stark reminder of how vulnerable the economy is to sudden surges in energy prices.

Our immense consumption of energy has made us highly dependent on foreign oil. In the 1950s we pumped all the oil we needed, but in the years following, we began to import more and more of the oil we need. Today we import 55 percent of the oil we consume, and analysts expect that number to rise to 65 percent by 2020. Nearly half of our oil imports come from OPEC, the Organization of the Petroleum Exporting Countries. Oil exploration in pristine areas of Alaska and elsewhere would not significantly reduce this shortfall. The only realistic explanation from the Bush administration's aggressive efforts to allow oil drilling in the Arctic National Wildlife Refuge is that it cares more about pandering to Big Oil than protecting this magnificent environmental treasure.

We cannot allow ourselves to remain dependent for oil on foreign nations, some of whom have values and interests that are hostile to ours. Globalization has made energy conservation even more important. As nations such as China dramatically increase their use of energy, we will all be competing for the same limited world supply. Costs will be driven up for each of us, our economy will be weakened, and the world will suffer unsustainable levels of pollution.

Shamefully, we have no serious policy in place to reduce our energy consumption or invest in new environmental technology. The president's 2005 oil exploration plan was completely inadequate for this age of rapidly growing energy use on a planet whose environment is at risk.

It is long past time to crack down on auto emissions. In

1975, U.S. cars averaged fourteen miles a gallon. The OPEC oil embargo of the time stimulated technological innovations, and ten years later the average car got twenty-eight miles per gallon. Today the average has dropped to about twenty miles a gallon. We are driving in reverse.

We also lag behind in the development of cheaper alternative fuels. We invented the solar power industry, but Japan now controls nearly 45 percent of that market.

A sound energy conservation policy should include the following steps:

■ Raise fuel efficiency and emissions standards for automobiles, buses, and trucks.

■ Reduce power plant emissions.

■ Set stricter standards of energy efficiency for furnaces and other appliances.

■ Offer new incentives for the development of better technologies and manufacturing processes to produce hybrid cars and other fuel-efficient vehicles.

■ Invest substantially in alternative forms of energy, especially renewable sources such as solar, biomass, and wind energy.

■ Link energy conservation initiatives to greater investments in mass transit.

An additional benefit of such a policy is that it will create more good jobs in America. The Apollo Alliance, a consortium of businesses, labor unions, environmental organizations, and think tanks, estimates that investing $5 billion a year in renewable energy and associated activities would generate more than 900,000 good new jobs in the next ten years. Investing $3 billion a year in fuel-efficient automobiles would generate nearly 130,000 good jobs over the same period.

According to the Alliance, a serious plan for energy conservation would ultimately pay for itself in higher productivity, additional jobs, and lower costs. It would also reduce our oil imports by one to two million barrels a day—equal to what we now import from the Middle East. It would reduce carbon and other emissions, and ease the distortions of our foreign policy caused by our ties to oil-producing nations in the Middle East.

Transportation and Communications

We cannot separate our transportation policy from our energy policy, nor can we neglect it in the age of globalization. Transportation issues are complex, and federal, state, and local policies must be well coordinated. Congestion in eighty-three major metropolitan areas now costs the nation $83 billion a year in lost time. Better roads would help, but public transit is more efficient and saves energy costs. We must invest in public transit systems, fast trains, and effective urban and suburban planning. As international trade becomes a larger share of our economy, transporting goods efficiently will be increasingly important.

Our communications infrastructure also requires attention. With the Internet now indispensable, we cannot have a nation of haves and have-nots. Personal computers and Internet connections must be available to all Americans, especially the young. We cannot afford to fall behind in the use of broadband and other new communication technologies.

Almost certainly, intelligent public investments in transportation and communications will produce major returns for the economy and for our future. They are costs in a technical sense, but they are also an assurance that our standard of living will grow. They are investments that create jobs and make our economy more productive at the same time.

Research and Development

The physical sciences were the engines of economic growth and improved living standards in the twentieth century, and the life sciences can fill the same role in this new century. America is a world leader in research in these areas, and we must maintain that advantage. But it is not certain that we will.

The past century brought the development of commercial electric power, the automobile, the airplane, atomic power, and the computer. Our understanding of the universe in which we live grew by more in that century than in all of prior history, and discoveries in the life sciences may well shape the next century as profoundly.

Continuing to be at the forefront of the life sciences may

well be the most important way for America to retain its leadership in the world economy in coming years. The opportunities for a better life for all will be boundless. We are entering a golden age of health care, in which researchers, for the first time, are truly beginning to understand the basic mechanisms of all diseases.

We may soon see dramatic breakthroughs in cures for inherited diseases such as cystic fibrosis, juvenile diabetes, and sickle-cell anemia. New biomaterials will replace damaged organs. A scarred cornea may not mean blindness. A crushed spine may not mean a lifetime in a wheelchair. We may soon know how to repair birth defects before a baby is born.

Politics has intruded, however, on scientific research. President Bush has already imposed restrictions on stem cell research. Public health agencies, notably the Food and Drug Administration, suffer from the taint of politicization. As we decode the human genome, new issues of civil rights are being raised that must be addressed according to America's highest values. The progress of science must not be threatened unless it interferes with clear and unmistakable dangers to health or other basic rights.

Today, however, basic research is in danger, even as it is laying the foundation for the great breakthroughs of our time. Total R&D spending in America remains strong, but private industries are conducting a much higher proportion of the research than in the past, and their focus is on immediate payoffs. The federal government, which once focused primarily on basic research, also now focuses more on its applications. A key agency for scientific investment has long been the Defense

Department, but it reduced that funding from 3.3 percent of its spending in 1994 to 1.9 percent in 2004. With these cutbacks, we may well be sacrificing our lead in producing the future great breakthroughs of this century. In addition, as we invest more in research in the life sciences, research in the physical sciences, mathematics, and engineering has stopped growing.

To deal with these problems, some experts say we should triple our R&D spending over the next decade. We have the government institutions and sophisticated universities to exploit such an investment. We cannot be the leading economy in a world of advancing technology without such a commitment. Revitalizing education and public investment in America can transform globalization from a current threat to a future golden opportunity.

Discouraging the Offshoring of Jobs

We must also counteract incentives in today's economy that encourage businesses to ship work abroad in search of lower-wage employees. Some in America use globalization in selfish and shortsighted ways, at the expense of their workers and the nation's long-term growth. American corporations operating overseas enjoy large tax breaks under our tax laws. Sometimes they pay no corporate income tax at all. Such abuses encourage them to locate their operations and facilities overseas and send U.S. jobs abroad. We should end these tax advantages and use the funds saved to give tax relief to companies that raise employment at home. We should provide a new job creation tax credit for any company that expands its workforce in America. These incentives could be similar to the tax subsidies we currently provide to encourage investment in new equipment. Why should we encourage job-saving investment in equipment without providing a similar benefit to firms that create good jobs at home?

In the 1980s I was involved in developing federal rules that required firms to notify workers when plants are about to be closed. We need something similar for offshoring. We should require corporations that send substantial numbers of U.S. jobs overseas to provide a community impact statement similar to current environmental impact statements. These statements would tell us whether new job opportunities are available in the community, whether job training is available, and whether the offshoring is needed to protect the company's finances. Such information would give us a clearer understanding of the true costs and benefits of offshoring, and U.S. companies would be encouraged to reevaluate their decisions as they become more aware of their full impact and ramifications.

Expanding the Safety Net

Technological change and global competition have made many American jobs obsolete. The problem is not the fault of the employees, but when it occurs, they lose not only their jobs but also their health benefits, and often their pension benefits. If they find a new job, it is usually for significantly lower pay. It makes sense to allow American firms to compete freely. But we must also protect American workers from the burdens of this more competitive and more flexible world economy. Unemployment benefits should be increased, and should be granted for longer periods of time. Effective job-training programs should be available to help workers qualify for available jobs. What is needed is a national employment agency to match workers and available jobs. Survival of the fittest is not an acceptable strategy. We must help firms take advantage of globalization, but we must also protect those who become its innocent victims.

Improving International Cooperation

It is also vital to protect our businesses as they compete in a global environment in which flexibility, creativity, and rapid response matter. It is unfair to require firms in the United States to compete under tax and regulatory disadvantages compared to foreign firms. We should be striving for global environmental standards, labor standards, and standards against corruption so that honest American businesses are not placed at unfair disadvantages when competing with businesses in other countries that do not require high standards.

In addition, we should strengthen international agreements to prevent other nations and rogue companies from copying our technologies without meeting basic copyright standards. The protection of intellectual property rights is more important than ever for our competitiveness as the world becomes smaller. Our strength in the global economy will come from our innovations, and the profits from those innovations are essential for the continued growth of our economy and the good jobs of the future. Whether the issue is new computer technologies, break-throughs in medicine, or blockbuster movies, we must protect those innovations from modern-day pirates who reproduce them without compensating those who developed them.

In meeting the challenges of a shrinking world we should not, however, lower our standards to meet those of other nations. We should make every effort to raise the standards of other nations. Our goal should be uniform international business rules on labor, the environment, accounting, and procurement. We must demand a level playing field for all, and we should include such provisions in our trade agreements. We should encourage the International Labor Organization to strengthen its role in overseeing labor standards throughout the world. United States support for these efforts would make a significant difference.

Raising labor standards in other nations would help them develop stronger economies too. Employee safety, a realistic minimum wage, limitations on child labor, and a commitment to retirement security would plant the seeds of a thriving middle class around the world, generate greater demand for the goods and services needed to do so, and reduce the poverty, despair, and anger that breed terrorism.

Yet another goal should be honest and open accounting, which would make businesses everywhere more efficient. The free and open flow of information is a cornerstone of good capitalism. After World War II the developed nations of the world came together to form financial, currency, and trade agreements that helped produce an era of great prosperity. We can do the same again.

Today, however, intensifying global competition is taking the world dangerously close to abandoning the standards that have made business so successful in the developed world. In America, the Progressive Era brought the reforms needed to create a strong middle class and assure a fair economy. By protecting the rights of labor, raising taxes, broadening voting rights, and creating a central bank, those reforms contributed significantly to economic growth. The new world economy is at a similar stage today. Globalization presents huge opportunities, much as our own economy did at the end of the nineteenth century. But these opportunities can be realized only through adequate international accords, and America should be a leader in this effort.

CHAPTER FOUR

Creating an Economy for All

"Equality was in fact the most radical and most powerful ideological force let loose in the Revolution," writes the historian Gordon Wood. "Once invoked, the idea of equality could not be stopped, and it tore through American society and culture with awesome power." Sixty years after the Revolution, Alexis de Tocqueville, the astute French observer of our society, wrote that nothing in the United States "struck me more forcibly than the equality of social conditions."

Some fifteen years later the author of *Moby-Dick* may have reached the heart of the ideal. Equality brings "democratic dignity," Herman Melville wrote, even to "the arm that wields a pick or drives a spike."

Equality is one of America's oldest and greatest promises. The nation's founders believed it was a self-evident truth that all persons are created equal, and they stated that fundamental principle in the opening words of the second paragraph of the Declaration of Independence. In our early years the right to equality did not extend to all Americans. But the idea itself unleashed energy that was unparalleled. No society, wrote Wood, was ever more egalitarian.

By equality, we never meant leveling society. We will

never begrudge anyone the opportunity to make a fortune. But all should be rewarded fairly for their efforts and abilities and have the opportunity to develop those abilities. Equality is the source of American optimism, of our civic life, of our participation in the political process, of access to education, of retirement security for all, and of protection from the general vagaries of life.

But in recent years society has become increasingly unequal. Not only the poor but also middle-income Americans find themselves falling further and further behind. Inequality results in inadequate health care, or in no health care at all. It means less access to education. Those with less have to pay the price when we do not invest enough in education or provide decent child care, or when the costs of prescription drugs rises to unconscionable levels. Inequality makes it harder for parents to balance work and family, because they must often accept low-wage jobs with long and irregular hours and little job security.

It is no surprise that those who earn less vote less, and that so many Americans do not trust public and private institutions. They justifiably blame government for their frustrations, because government no longer works for all the way it should. They know the promise of America is being broken.

In the past, when the economy failed to work for all, we responded as a nation. When the Industrial Revolution took hold in the nineteenth century and America became more unequal, the Progressive Era was the nation's response. In the devastating Great Depression, government again rose to the challenge, and the New Deal of Franklin Roosevelt and the Fair Deal of Harry Truman were its response. Now we must respond again.

President Kennedy said more than forty years ago that a rising tide lifts all boats, and there was good reason to believe he was right. His New Frontier led to the longest uninterrupted period of economic growth and price stability in our history up to that time. The economy grew rapidly in the 1960s, and people's incomes grew rapidly with it. The typical family earned twice as much in 1973 as it did in 1947. Incomes of those at the top, the bottom, and the middle rose together.

Over the past thirty years, however, the average wage paid to nonmanagerial workers in America has fallen, when adjusted for inflation. Family incomes have risen only modestly for an entire generation, and only because wives have gone to work in ever greater numbers. For many families, earnings have fallen. The incomes of minorities remain far below those of whites. Women still make less than men for the same work.

By contrast, CEOs have done magnificently for themselves. Today they earn three times what they did in the early 1990s, adjusted for inflation. They make an average of 135 times what their average employee makes. Twenty-five years ago they made only 25 times what their average workers made.

The wealthy did well when my brother was president, and their rising tide carried the entire nation with it. The top-earning 1 percent of Americans earned about 10 percent of the total income earned by all Americans. Today, that 1 percent has doubled their share—they now earn 20 percent of total American income. I never imagined when I became a senator that income inequality would return to the levels of 1929, but that is exactly what has happened.

Some leaders claim inequality is good for the nation. It

makes lower-income people work harder, they say, because they see how well the economy rewards others. It gives them incentives to try to do better themselves and earn more. But today's economy refutes that claim. The poverty rate is up. We have more children living in poverty than any other nation in the developed world. Middle-income families are under constant strain, because their basic costs have risen far faster than their income, even when both parents work. Such costs include providing higher education for their children, living in neighborhoods with first-class public schools, maintaining adequate health insurance, or buying a car. It is time to stop making excuses and make sure the economy works for all of us again.

How Unequal Is America?

Family incomes are the best measure of our standard of living. As Figure 2 (see page 107) indicates, between 1947 and 1973 the incomes of most families rose together. Those in the bottom 20 percent almost doubled their income, as did all other income groups. In fact, their incomes rose slightly faster than those in the top 5 percent.

Later, especially in the 1980s, inequality began to grow, and it has continued to do so. Only during the prosperous years in the late 1990s, under President Clinton, did inequality stop expanding. As Figure 3 (see page 107) shows, family incomes among richer groups grew faster than among middle-income groups and the poor between 1979 and 2004. Those in the top 5 percent increased their incomes by more than 40 percent, while those in the bottom 20 percent increased their incomes only slightly.

These incomes were measured before taxes. But our tax system has not made America more equal. The income tax is still progressive, but less so than in the past. The Earned Income Tax Credit benefits many low-income families. But for the vast majority of our people, the payroll tax subtracted from their wages each week to pay for Medicare and Social Security is the biggest tax they pay, and it is a regressive tax—no matter how large your income, you pay the same percentage tax rate, and income greater than $94,200 a year is not subject to the Social Security payroll tax at all.

Some economists claim that people are rising out of lower income levels more rapidly now than before. But the evidence shows they are not. Despite the American promise, children born to parents in the bottom 20 percent of income have only a little better than a one in fifteen chance of reaching the top 20 percent in their lifetime. Especially disturbing is the fact that those born in the middle 20 percent are more likely to sink to the bottom than rise to the top, and those at the top are more likely to remain there.

The poor and minorities bear the greatest burdens. The unemployment rate for African American men is twice the rate for white men, regardless of their level of education, and the unemployment rate for Hispanic Americans is similarly high. The gap in pay between men and women also remains wide.

Health and pension benefits on the job are also unequal. Three out of four workers whose wages rank them in the top 20 percent have private health insurance, but only one out of

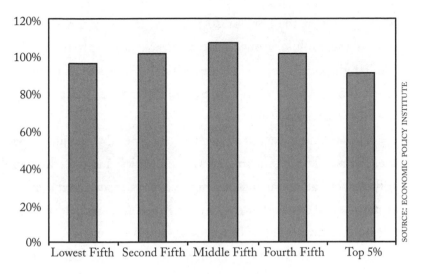

Figure 2. **Percentage Change in Median Family Income**
1947–1973 (adjusted for inflation)

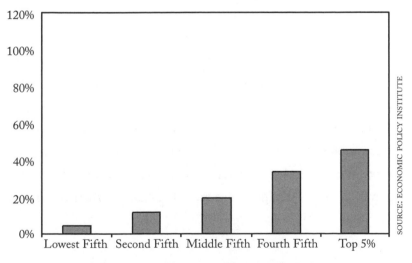

Figure 3. **Percentage Change in Median Family Income**
1979–2004 (adjusted for inflation)

four workers in the bottom 20 percent, and only three out of five in the middle group, have insurance through their job. Similar disparities disadvantage African American, Hispanic American, and female employees, and the same disparities exist in pension coverage.

If we measure wealth instead of income, the inequality is even worse. The net worth of whites, which includes homes and financial assets such as savings accounts, stocks, and bonds, averages eight times that of African Americans and more than twenty-five times that of Hispanic Americans.

Home ownership is the major source of wealth. Of those in the top half of earners in America, eight in ten own homes, but among those in the bottom half, only five in ten own homes. Similar disparities exist in minority home ownership.

When people don't earn what they should, their frustration rises. They don't feel the American dream applies to them. The incomes of a high proportion of working men actually fell, even as they grew more experienced over any twenty-year period since the 1970s. A fifty-year-old worker often earns less than he made when he was thirty and had far less experience and fewer skills.

People seek explanations and sometimes scapegoats for such frustrations. It is no surprise that they take it out on government when they have been told repeatedly, ever since President Reagan took office, that government is the cause of their problems.

How to Make the Economy Work for All:
The First Step Is a Strong Economy

We relearned an important lesson during the economic boom in the second half of the 1990s under President Clinton. We learned that it is still possible to have a growing economy in which everyone thrives together. In fact, during those years, the family incomes in each 20 percent grew at about the same fairly rapid rate, comparable to the rates from 1947 to 1973. The family incomes of African Americans and Hispanic Americans actually grew even faster than the incomes of white families.

But in the past five years, as we slowly recovered from the 2001 recession, the poorest Americans—and even the middle class—have been left out of the recovery. Wages have stagnated, incomes have fallen, and working families have been squeezed from many directions. Gasoline prices have risen 37 percent since 2001. Housing costs are up 49 percent. Health costs have risen 52 percent, and college costs have increased 46 percent. Countless families now teeter on piles of bills and are increasingly worried about the future.

President Bush's large tax cuts have contributed significantly to these problems. Most of the tax reductions went to the wealthy, and they did not spend enough of their windfall to give the economy the stimulus it needed. If the Bush tax cuts are made permanent, as the president wants, the red ink that will flow will further undermine the nation.

It was the height of irresponsibility to cut taxes in wartime the way President Bush did. The danger is compounded by the fact that beginning in 2008, the post–World War II baby boom generation will begin to retire, and their demands on the economy will rise significantly. Businesses are as insecure as households, and wary about hiring more workers or taking on other long-term costs.

Some claim incorrectly that at least the unemployment rate is low. But the rate fails to reflect the large number of workers who have stopped seeking jobs. If the same proportion was looking for work now as in the late 1990s, the unemployment rate would be a disturbing 7 percent. No amount of happy talk by the president can dispel all the concerns of both business and labor about the troubled state of today's economy.

The Minimum Wage

Few policies tell more about a nation than how it treats those at the bottom. As Hurricane Katrina vividly and sadly reminded us, vast numbers of people in America have been forgotten. Millions across the nation can't afford the rising cost of higher education, so they don't send their children to college. They can't afford the rising cost of prescription drugs, so they don't take the drugs they need. They can't afford to see a doctor when they feel ill, so they wait for a medical emergency to seek care.

110

They could not afford a car, so they were left defenseless in the path of Hurricane Katrina in 2005.

Most of these men and women work hard, but their wages don't begin to enable them to make ends meet. I have spoken with people who earn the minimum wage and go without dinner so their children can eat and they can pay the rent. If not, they'd be evicted, and they could easily become homeless.

Since President Bush took office, more than 5 million more Americans are living in poverty. Thirty-seven million live below the poverty line, and more than 15 million live at less than half that line. Our poverty rate is substantially higher than in other industrial nations. Poverty in America is not just an economic issue. It is also a civil rights issue, since poverty rates for women, African Americans, and Hispanic Americans are significantly higher than for whites. It is a children's issue, since the number of children living in poverty has been increasing in recent years, after declining in the late 1990s. Today nearly one in five American children lives in poverty. Almost 14 million children go to bed hungry at night, not knowing where their next meal is coming from.

The federal minimum wage was enacted in 1938 as part of President Roosevelt's New Deal, to mitigate the heavy toll on millions of working families suffering from extreme poverty during the Great Depression. As Figure 5 (see pages 114–115) shows, the series of three increases enacted in 1938 for the years 1938–1940 nearly doubled the value of the minimum wage as a percentage of the poverty level at the time.

Through periodic increases over the next three decades under Democratic and Republican administrations alike, the nation

111

achieved one of the fundamental goals of a just society, which is that no one who works for a living should have to live in poverty. But the tide has turned since 1968. The minimum wage has not kept pace with inflation. It has not been raised at all in the past nine years, and such workers have again fallen below the poverty level. Eighteen states and the District of Columbia have tried in recent years to close the gap by increasing the minimum wage for their own workers. Those states contain half the nation's total workforce, but the other half has not benefited at all.

Today the minimum wage is $5.15 an hour. Adjusted for inflation (see Figure 4, opposite), its purchasing power is now at its lowest level since 1948, and is barely half the level at its peak in 1968. President Johnson's Great Society has been cut in half and minimum wage workers continue to fall further and further behind.

Workers earning the minimum wage cannot get by in today's economy. Those who put in forty hours a week, fifty-two weeks a year, will earn $10,712 this year. For a single parent with two children, that amount is only 67 percent of the poverty level.

The entire annual pay of a full-time minimum wage worker is less than the annual premium for an average family's health insurance. It is not enough to afford the rent on a two-bedroom apartment in any area of the nation. In Wyoming, a minimum wage worker would have to work 83 hours a week to pay the rent on such an apartment. In Louisiana, it would take 88 hours; in Arizona, 112 hours; in Massachusetts, 130 hours.

To make the economy work for all, the minimum wage must be raised substantially as soon as possible. An increase to $7.25 an hour, which I favor but which the Republican Congress

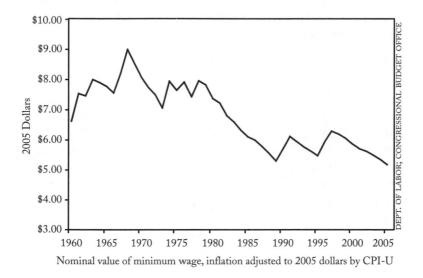

Nominal value of minimum wage, inflation adjusted to 2005 dollars by CPI-U

Figure 4. **The Declining Value of the Minimum Wage**

continues to reject, would increase the annual pay of a full-time worker by $4,400 a year, or about $85 a week, and bring it within 6 percent of the poverty level again.

Think what that income would mean. It could pay for more than a year of groceries, or nine months of rent, or a year and a half of heat and electricity, or almost two years of child care, or full tuition at a community college. It could have helped more than 490,000 workers in the Gulf region after Hurricane Katrina.

Opponents claim that a raise in the minimum wage would harm the economy by reducing the number of jobs. But in 1996, the last time Congress acted to raise the federal minimum wage—to $4.75 for that year and to $5.15 for 1996—an economic boom followed. Millions of jobs a year were created, the unemployment rate fell to its lowest level since the 1960s, and wages rose at all income levels.

113

Year	Minimum Wage in Dollars per Hour	Minimum Wage in 2005 Dollars	Minimum Wage as % of Poverty Line for Family of Three
1938	$0.25	$3.46	45%
1939	$0.30	$4.22	54%
1940	$0.40	$5.58	72%
1941	$0.40	$5.31	69%
1942	$0.40	$4.79	62%
1943	$0.40	$4.52	58%
1944	$0.40	$4.44	57%
1945	$0.40	$4.34	56%
1946	$0.40	$4.01	52%
1947	$0.40	$3.50	45%
1948	$0.40	$3.24	42%
1949	$0.75	$6.15	80%
1950	$0.75	$6.08	79%
1951	$0.75	$5.63	73%
1952	$0.75	$5.53	71%
1953	$0.75	$5.49	71%
1954	$0.75	$5.45	70%
1955	$1.00	$7.29	94%
1956	$1.00	$7.18	93%
1957	$1.00	$6.95	90%
1958	$1.00	$6.76	87%
1959	$1.00	$6.71	87%
1960	$1.00	$6.60	85%
1961	$1.15	$7.51	97%
1962	$1.15	$7.44	96%
1963	$1.25	$7.98	103%
1964	$1.25	$7.88	102%
1965	$1.25	$7.75	100%
1966	$1.25	$7.53	97%
1967	$1.40	$8.19	106%
1968	$1.60	$8.98	116%
1969	$1.60	$8.51	110%
1970	$1.60	$8.05	104%

Figure 5. The Minimum Wage and Poverty

Year	Minimum Wage in Dollars per Hour	Minimum Wage in 2005 Dollars	Minimum Wage as % of Poverty Line for Family of Three
1971	$1.60	$7.72	100%
1972	$1.60	$7.48	97%
1973	$1.60	$7.04	91%
1974	$2.00	$7.92	102%
1975	$2.10	$7.62	99%
1976	$2.30	$7.89	102%
1977	$2.30	$7.41	96%
1978	$2.65	$7.94	103%
1979	$2.90	$7.80	101%
1980	$3.10	$7.35	95%
1981	$3.35	$7.20	93%
1982	$3.35	$6.78	88%
1983	$3.35	$6.57	85%
1984	$3.35	$6.30	81%
1985	$3.35	$6.08	79%
1986	$3.35	$5.97	77%
1987	$3.35	$5.76	74%
1988	$3.35	$5.53	71%
1989	$3.35	$5.28	68%
1990	$3.80	$5.68	73%
1991	$4.25	$6.09	79%
1992	$4.25	$5.92	76%
1993	$4.25	$5.74	74%
1994	$4.25	$5.60	72%
1995	$4.25	$5.45	70%
1996	$4.75	$5.91	76%
1997	$5.15	$6.27	81%
1998	$5.15	$6.17	80%
1999	$5.15	$6.04	78%
2000	$5.15	$5.84	76%
2001	$5.15	$5.68	73%
2002	$5.15	$5.59	72%
2003	$5.15	$5.47	71%
2004	$5.15	$5.32	69%
2005	$5.15	$5.15	67%

Opponents also claim that increasing the minimum wage won't help working families, because only teenagers earn the minimum wage. In fact, almost two thirds of such workers are adults. A third are working mothers. More than a third are the sole breadwinners in their family.

Year after year Congress refuses to raise the minimum wage, but it does not hesitate to give its own members raise after raise in our already substantial six-figure salaries. The Speaker of the House says that members of Congress deserve such raises "to be able to keep up with the cost of living, so that they can take care of their families and provide for their families like everybody else." In fact, Congress has raised its own pay by more than $31,000 since the last minimum wage increase, but not even a penny increase for the working poor?

Raising the minimum wage was not a partisan issue in the past. It was raised under every Democratic president since FDR. It was also raised under Republican presidents Dwight Eisenhower, Gerald Ford, and the first President Bush. It must be raised again now, and raised substantially.

Giving Employees a Voice at Work

Historically, our economy has been more equal when workers have a strong voice at their workplaces. The ability to organize, choose a union, and bargain collectively gives employees the power to insist on a fair share of the profits derived from their hard work.

It is no coincidence that wages were rising in parallel with profits and economic growth at the height of union membership in the mid-1950s. Today, only 12 percent of private-sector workers have union representation, and wages have been stagnant in the face of economic growth and soaring corporate profits.

It's little wonder that the majority of American workers want union representation. Union wages are 27 percent higher than nonunion wages; 93 percent of union members are covered by health insurance; 76 percent of union members have paid sick leave.

The landmark National Labor Relations Act was enacted as part of President Roosevelt's New Deal seventy years ago in order to protect the rights of workers to organize and bargain collectively with their employer for decent wages, benefits, and working conditions. However, subsequent changes in the law, restrictive court decisions, lax enforcement, and the rapid growth of powerful anti-union consulting firms have all undermined the ability of workers to use the law for its intended purpose.

Employers increasingly resort to illegal tactics to coerce and intimidate those who attempt to organize unions. Employees who join the fight for workers' rights are harassed or fired. Recent studies show that employers illegally fire workers one out of every four times when they try to form a union.

These abuses are prohibited by the law, but the fines for violations are so weak that employers have no incentive to avoid unlawful behavior. They simply treat the fines as a cost of doing business. Even when employers are penalized more heavily, the remedies for harmed employees come too late. It can take years before a fired union supporter receives back pay or reinstatement from the National Labor Relations Board. Workers who seek to organize are not adequately protected, and the obstacles to unionization in the face of well-organized campaigns of business opposition are rarely surmountable.

The time has come to end this rampant abuse of millions of employees. We must level the playing field again and restore greater equality to our economy. Employees deserve the right to organize without facing coercion or intimidation. Better protections will enable employees to organize freely and negotiate fairly. Stronger and quicker penalties for violations by employers will put real teeth into the National Labor Relations Act.

Equality in our society requires a vital labor movement so that employees can stand up for their rights and benefit fairly from the fruits of their work. America owes its hardworking men and women no less.

Fairness in Taxes

A century ago America debated whether a progressive income tax was just. Those who earn more, President Theodore Roosevelt and many others insisted, should pay a higher propor-tion of their income in support of the nation. They won that debate, and so did America. The Sixteenth Amendment was adopted in 1913. The principle of income taxation was protected by the Constitution, and the nation embarked on a period of rapid economic growth. The middle class was born in our society.

Since the 1970s, however, our tax system has become significantly less progressive. Income tax rates have been broadly reduced, and regressive taxes, notably the payroll tax, have been raised. President Bush's deep tax cuts have made the nation's tax system even more regressive. The share of federal taxes paid by the wealthiest 1 percent of Americans has fallen more sharply for them than for the rest of our citizens.

In a time of already extraordinary income inequality, it is especially unfair to bestow lavish new tax breaks on the wealthy. Americans do not want a tax code in which average citizens pay twice as much tax on their weekly wages as millionaires pay on their stock market gains.

The Bush tax cuts also have dug America into a dangerously deep financial hole. They have already cost the nation $2 trillion in lost tax revenues, with additional large losses still to come. For a Republican administration and a Republican Congress supposedly committed to fiscal responsibility, the acceptance of the huge deficits brought on by their massive tax reductions is breathtaking hypocrisy.

We should reverse the tax breaks for the wealthy enacted under President Bush, but preserve and expand the reductions for middle-income and lower-income working Americans.

We should restore as soon as possible the rates of the three highest tax brackets to their pre-2001 levels, which were 39.6 percent, 36 percent, and 31 percent until they were reduced under President Bush.

It is hardly unfair to ask the wealthiest to pay the same tax rates they paid during the economic boom of the 1990s. Republicans cried foul when President Clinton raised rates in 1993. It would undermine investment, they said. Entrepreneurship would be crushed and talented leaders in the private sector would not work as hard. The critics were wrong then, and they would be wrong again. Our current exploding deficits would be reduced significantly.

A critical reexamination of so-called tax expenditures is also long overdue. Another prime example of breathtaking Republican hypocrisy is their eagerness to cut any and all direct federal spending for social programs while they adamantly resist any scrutiny of the hundreds of billions of dollars of federal funds spent each year through the backdoor of the tax code in the form of tax credits and tax deductions. By any realistic definition, these are government spending programs too, yet they receive virtually no scrutiny. We must identify those that support real needs and those that are wasteful. These tax expenditures also raise serious questions of equity, since tax deductions are worth the most to those with the most income. We can save a great deal of money if we examine tax expenditures more carefully and end unjustifiable programs.

Modernizing Workplace Laws

The unemployment insurance system was created to support families during hard times. It is also an important factor for the economy. In fact, former Treasury Secretary Robert Rubin has called it the "almost perfect economic stimulus." Workers who have paid into the unemployment insurance system receive modest payments after being laid off. Typically, they spend these funds quickly, helping their families survive, which provides a useful jump start when the economy is weak.

When President Reagan was in office, the unemployment rate rose to historically high levels. Yet his administration actually cut back significantly on unemployment insurance coverage and unfairly characterized this important social program as a "prepaid vacation for freeloaders."

Changes in the labor market have also made reform essential. A higher proportion of workers today are employed part-time or as temporary workers and are not protected by unemployment insurance at all. Workers who lose their jobs in today's economy find it far more difficult to obtain new work. Twice as many Americans as in the 1970s are now unemployed for six months or longer. When they finally obtain new jobs, they must often take substantial pay cuts, which now average eight thousand dollars a year.

To fulfill its important purpose, unemployment insurance should be expanded to cover many more workers. Part-time, temporary, and low-wage employees should be covered, and the level of payments should rise.

Other workplace reforms are also needed, such as protecting overtime pay for hardworking employees. In 2004, the Bush administration cruelly and unilaterally modified the eligibility criteria for such pay, denying overtime protection to more than 6 million Americans, including nurses, cooks, clerical workers, nursery school teachers, and many others. Since firms no longer have to give these workers extra pay for overtime, employers have an incentive to demand longer hours. As a result, large numbers of these men and women are now being required by their employer to work more hours for less pay, and they have even less time to spend with their families. Overtime protections need to be restored for these millions of employees. The forty-hour workweek is still vital to American family life.

Protecting workplace safety must also be put back on the agenda. After the Occupational Safety and Health Act became law in 1970, the rate of injuries and fatalities on the job declined. But there is still a long way to go. Fifteen workers are killed and twelve thousand more are injured each day. Parents who have lost children in workplace accidents have pleaded with me to act.

The heart of the problem is that many companies ignore the law but are rarely held accountable. Penalties are so low that prosecutors do not find it worthwhile to pursue violations.

In another anti-worker action, soon after taking office the Bush administration rescinded rules adopted under President Clinton's administration to protect employees from ergonomic injuries. No serious person doubts such injuries exist. The National Academy of Sciences estimates that 1 million men and women lost time at work in 2005 because of such injuries, at a cost to the economy of $50 billion.

Congress cannot continue to ignore this shameful situation. Our inadequate workplace health and safety rules demand reform now.

Retirement Security

One of the nation's proudest social accomplishments of the last century was to make decent retirement possible for the elderly. But in the past two decades this security has eroded badly.

Private pensions are no longer certain. More and more workers have to bear the risk of financing their retirement through pension plans whose payments depend on how well they have invested. Social Security's deepest principles are now under attack. An economy that once worked for all is in danger of not working for tens of millions of retirees in coming years.

Social Security was created under President Franklin Roosevelt as the centerpiece of his New Deal reforms, and no government program better reflects the values of the American people. As a nation we are a community that takes care of our most vulnerable members, and Social Security is the bedrock example of this commitment. Two out of every three retirees receive more than half their income from Social Security. Without their guaranteed monthly benefit check, most of them would be living in poverty today.

In fact, Social Security does much more than guarantee retirement income for the elderly. It also provides lifetime disability insurance for those who become seriously injured or ill. When a worker with children dies, Social Security provides financial support for them until they become adults. In many ways, Social Security is the ultimate safety net, and it has been hugely successful.

It is not a handout but an earned benefit, financed by workers through a payroll tax on their wages during their working lives. It is the most cost-effective and affordable way for most Americans to obtain disability insurance, survivors' benefits for their children, and an inflation-adjusted annuity to finance their retirement. It is remarkably efficient—its administration costs total less than 1 percent of all the benefits paid. It has worked well for seventy years, and it will continue to work well for future generations as long as we hold true to the fundamental American values it embodies.

Its success helps explain why benefits for the elderly have been expanded in the past by Democrats and Republicans alike. President Eisenhower raised benefits significantly. President Nixon indexed benefits so that they now rise with inflation. Under President Reagan, payroll taxes were increased to keep the system solvent.

Another course correction is obviously needed today. The ratio of current workers to beneficiaries will fall as baby boomers retire, making it harder to finance the program.

The greatest threat to the future of Social Security, however, is from those who seek to dismantle it in the guise of saving it. With little success, the Bush administration has waged a long campaign of half truths and false alarms in a craven effort to convince the public that Social Security is on the verge of bankruptcy and cannot be sustained.

Their crass antigovernment ideological goal was to privatize Social Security. The American people understood right away that the Bush plan would take the "security" out of Social Security and leave senior citizens at the mercy of the stock market to finance their retirement.

The plan was so obviously unacceptable that it went nowhere. But we must maintain our vigilance. No imminent financial crisis is facing Social Security. The program will remain on solid ground for decades to come. It has sufficient finances to pay full benefits for the next forty years or more. After that, it could pay at least 74 percent of scheduled benefits.

The challenge, therefore, is to provide Social Security with enough additional revenue to pay full benefits beyond the next forty years, and we can do so without fundamental changes. Dismantling Social Security would betray our most fundamental values as a nation. We cannot let it happen.

We must also take action to make private pensions more secure. In recent years we've seen example after example of corporate abuse. CEOs arrange enormous sweetheart pensions for themselves, their companies collapse, and employees lose most of their retirement savings. We cannot tolerate a system in which executives of Enron cashed out more than $1 billion of company stock, knowing the company was in trouble, while employees who had been encouraged to invest in the company's stock lost $1 billion of their savings, as well as their jobs and their health insurance.

Other dramatic examples have also been front-page news in recent years. Across America large numbers of corporations are breaking promises to employees by curtailing pension coverage. Firms have knowingly underfinanced their pension plans because accounting rules allow them to do so.

Pensions now offered by companies typically no longer guarantee specific monthly payments after retirement. Employers are shifting to new types of plans to which the company contributes, but employees are responsible for investing it. The risk is on the workers. Some will do well, others won't, and a decent retirement is no longer a sure thing.

Such programs are a harmful mirage. In America today

10 percent of Americans own 75 percent of stocks. When we grant tax benefits to those who can save more, we benefit the rich far more than the rest of America. The higher the tax bracket, and the more you can afford to save, the higher the benefit. The best way to increase savings is to pay workers more and remove the inequalities that plague so many in the lower portions of the income spectrum.

Conclusion

We can make the economy work for all again, but only with a determined effort which recognizes that the tables have turned against employees in America. Some experts suggest that growing inequality is a natural result of the revolution in technology. I refuse to believe that we cannot respond to such a change. Responsible government policies in the past succeeded in reducing inequality, and we can do so again.

To those who insist that inequality merely reflects the needs of the market, I say that America does not live by "survival of the fittest" alone, and never has. We created the greatest economy in the world because people believe it rewards their work fairly. Their confidence unleashed unprecedented levels of energy and originality, and also the courage to demand change. Ours is the greatest egalitarian society in the world. May it always be so.

CHAPTER FIVE

Guaranteeing
Health Care for Every American

L ike so many families, mine has not escaped the tragedy of disease or the pain of injury. As I look back I realize that these experiences have informed some of my deepest interests as a senator.

One of the most indelible of these experiences was with my sister Rosemary, who was born mentally retarded. She was my parents' first-born daughter, and they wanted to give her as normal a life as possible. She lived with our family for many years, and caring for her became the responsibility of us all. We lived with her disabilities day in and day out, and tried to make sense of why some people are healthy and others, through no fault of their own, are not. My parents' intense love and care for Rosemary was a lifelong lesson for the rest of us.

We lost my brother Joe during one of his courageous flying missions in World War II. Fortunately, Jack came home safely, after narrowly escaping death on his PT boat in the South Pacific. But he had a severe back injury and spent months recovering in the naval hospital nearby. His back plagued him for the rest of his life.

While campaigning in 1964, I was in a serious plane accident in Massachusetts, in which both the pilot and copilot were killed. My back was broken, and I spent six months in a Striker frame, being turned over every three hours. Thanks to fine doctors and nurses and the best possible medical care, I recovered.

Later, my father lived with the debilitating effects of a stroke for the last seven years of his life. My mother required constant attention as she grew older. Caring for them both, I began to understand the long-term-care issues that now consume the time and money of so many Americans.

You feel the pain of disease the most when it affects your children. Recently, my daughter Kara battled lung cancer. We consulted the best physicians we could find, and she has fully recovered. In the 1980s, my son Patrick had severe asthma. During treatment, doctors also discovered a tumor in his spinal column. He is now fine.

In the 1970s my son Teddy lost his leg to cancer, at the age of twelve. I left the Senate every third Friday to be with him for his chemotherapy sessions. My pay was not withheld by the Senate because of these absences. But the pay of other parents at those sessions often was. I met people who were mortgaging their homes and taking extra jobs to pay for these treatments. All they sought was a chance for their children. They risked personal bankruptcy even when there was no certainty that the treatments would succeed. Not all were lucky, but we were. Teddy is a healthy young adult today, a successful business consultant and one of the best sailors I have ever seen.

We were a fortunate family who learned the value of good health, and it is hard for me to accept that every American does not have the same first-rate care. A few years before Teddy's illness, I had become chairman of the Senate Health

Subcommittee. I began to devote much of my attention to providing all Americans with the protection of good health insurance, but I have fallen short of the goal. I've failed to convince my colleagues that far-reaching health reforms are essential. We have made some important gains, but we have not done enough.

No one in America should be denied the best medical treatment. For me, this principle should be as incontestable as our belief that our national defense benefits us all, not only those who pay the most taxes. We will all need medical care in our lives, because we will all be touched by illness or injury.

The great breakthroughs of medicine in recent years make creating the best and most efficient medical system in the world all the more important. No American should be deprived of these breakthroughs. We marvel at our ability to treat heart disease, asthma, depression, and other physical and psychological disorders. The routine replacement of limbs and other vital organs today is remarkable. As a result of these and so many other discoveries, our lives have been extended significantly. Fifty-year-olds today are expected to live well into their eighties because of medical advances and better preventive care. Since the 1800s, government has always helped encourage and fund the medical breakthroughs of science. Through public health systems, vaccination programs, and the pioneering social legislation of the 1960s, including Medicare and Medicaid, we have spread the blessings of better medical care to most of the population. Advances in this new century will be even more remarkable, and we must take steps now so that all Americans can enjoy them.

We have extraordinary talent—outstanding doctors and nurses, superb medical research, and state-of-the-art facilities. We already perform many tasks extremely well, but we know we can make the system much more efficient, minimize errors, improve treatments, restrain rising costs, and enhance the nation's overall health. As costs are brought under control, it will be less expensive to cover all Americans with adequate insurance. But we must begin to do so now.

One of the first problems we must solve is the high cost of care. Health spending is rising much faster than income. Under current policy, it will continue to do so, and the strain on our resources will only grow. Private and public spending on health care in America now totals more than 15 percent of our gross domestic product. Twenty years ago that figure was less than 10 percent. Ten years from now it is likely to be more than 20 percent.

As a result of these high costs, 45 million Americans, 17 percent of the population, have no health insurance. They are not old enough to qualify for Medicare, and they earn too much to qualify for Medicaid. Their employers don't offer coverage, and they can't afford to purchase it on their own. A typical family plan costs more for a year than a minimum wage worker's entire annual income. Four out of five of the uninsured work or belong to families in which a member works.

Studies show that no nation's system of health care is clearly superior to the others. Ours has many advantages over those of other nations, but others clearly have advantages over us. Other developed nations spend significantly less per person, or as a percentage of their economy, than we do. England, France, and

Canada spend 10 percent of their GDP on medical care, but America spends more than 15 percent.

Yet our infant mortality rate is high compared to the rates in other nations. Our average life spans are not nearly what they are in most of Europe. We are strong in caring for cancer patients but weak in caring for patients with asthma. We have made great progress against heart disease, but only half of the Americans who should be on beta blockers are given a prescription, and only half of those who receive a prescription actually take the drug. Such drugs reduce the risk of heart attack dramatically and are unquestionably vital for good care, but they are not reaching many of the people who need them. Other studies have documented that many procedures are overused, often the most expensive ones. Doctors who are well trained in complex procedures are eager to perform them, and they do.

There is no sign that under the current system the cost of health care will stop rising rapidly. The overall cost is staggering. Each 5 percent increase in the amount of GDP spent on health care comes to more than $550 billion—more than the cost of Social Security or our defense budget. It could easily cover energy independence for the nation, or pay for college and graduate school for all plus universal day care for young children, and still leave money to improve schools and pay for other essential programs.

The benefits of such health reform would be immense. Better health care means better and more productive workers. The economy would grow faster. If we are healthier as we grow older, we can work longer and more energetically. We can avoid needless personal tragedies, such as bankruptcy caused by medical costs. Half of all personal bankruptcies in America are the consequence of large medical bills.

Every citizen deserves the opportunity for a full and healthy life. It is unacceptable that so many millions of Americans today go without needed health care and live diminished lives because of it. Tragically, many of them are children.

If we have the will, we can solve these problems. We need a health care system that:

- protects all Americans;

- pays for all significant medical expenses;

- offers a choice of doctors to all Americans;

- ends the shameful disparities that undermine access to care and the quality of care for minorities;

- provides incentives for the most effective treatments, and disincentives for costly and unnecessary ones;

- emphasizes preventive medicine, including exercise, diet, reduced smoking and drinking, and regular checkups, screenings, and other diagnostic procedures;

- restrains the rising cost of prescription drugs;

- makes administrative record-keeping more efficient and less costly and makes maximum use of information technology to coordinate care, reduce errors, and minimize administrative expenses;

- eases the growing burden on businesses of providing health insurance for their employees; and

- invests fully in the National Institutes of Health, the source of so many of our most important medical breakthroughs.

This list is long, but we can accomplish much of it with a proposal I call Medicare for All. It would provide every American with high-quality and affordable health care, and enable all Americans to see the doctor of their choice. If organized properly, it would save administrative costs and keep pharmaceutical prices down. It would also greatly improve treatments by avoiding medical errors, covering those who now seek treatment only in emergencies, and providing realistic incentives for preventive care.

Preventive Care and Best Practices

A core principle of health reform must also be greater emphasis on preventive medicine, especially for children. The number of obese children has increased dramatically. In the 1960s, only 5 percent of our children aged six to nineteen were overweight, but today this is figure is 16 percent. Obese children are more likely to have asthma, and to suffer from diabetes and heart disease when they are older, with all the severe consequences those diseases can bring. Even diabetes in children is now on the rise, with debilitating consequences that include broken bones and seriously inflamed joints.

Studies of the relationship between television advertising and the increase in overweight children prove that modern marketing is harmful to children's diets. The food available in public schools is also a major concern. Food companies pay for sports programs and provide other subsidies to public schools in return for stocking school kitchens and corridors with their products. Nearly half of all elementary schools and almost all high schools now have vending machines that offer students easy access to soft drinks and snacks that raise their risk of obesity.

The nation must embark on a serious health education program to demonstrate the danger of poor diets to parents and their children. Local communities should be better informed about the dangers of the foods available in their schools and about how to curb easy access to them. Unless food companies voluntarily alter advertising that encourages poor diet practices, Congress must regulate it. Legislation to do so failed to pass in the 1980s, but childhood obesity is now far more serious, and Congress must act.

We must also encourage food companies to undertake new research to develop healthy food for children that is also tasty. A focus on children would also lead to a greater emphasis by parents on their own diets.

The irony is that although we're a first-world country, citizens in the third world eat healthier foods than we do. A prime culprit is our food industry, which finds it more profitable to market processed food than the actual commodities, such as by selling cereals with processed corn instead of unprocessed corn. Processed foods are often misleadingly sold as "health food" when the simple, unprocessed product is better for us.

Diet and exercise are only part of preventive health care. Reduced smoking and alcohol use have improved adult health, and reduced smoking by pregnant women has lowered infant mortality markedly.

In recent years researchers have also documented large gaps between what are widely regarded as the best medical practices and the typical medical practices used today. Closing these gaps will improve health and reduce costs as well. The Midwest Business Group on Health estimates that lost time from poor-quality care costs businesses two thousand dollars in higher health insurance premiums for every worker covered.

Examples of these gaps include the following:

- Patients with diabetes account for 10 percent of total health costs and a quarter of Medicare costs. Yet care that meets well-established standards has been shown to dramatically reduce complications from diabetes that result in amputations, blindness, and death. If we follow best practices, current costs could be reduced as much as 50 percent.

- Stroke is the third leading cause of death in the United States and also disables 2.5 million people annually. It accounts for $51 billion in costs each year. Appropriate and timely medical intervention with clot-dissolving drugs has been shown to reduce disability and death by 55 percent, but only a small number of patients actually receive such treatment.

- Congestive heart failure, the most common hospital diagnosis among the elderly, affects almost 5 million Americans and causes tens of thousands of deaths annually. More than $18 billion is spent each year for the care of these patients. Yet simple interventions, including good patient monitoring and case management, can reduce the costs of hospitalization by 75 percent.

- Arthritis and related rheumatic diseases are the leading causes of disability among adults. Every year they result in 750,000 hospitalizations, 39 million outpatient visits, and 4 million days of hospital care. Annual medical costs for these conditions total $51 billion, and additional losses in worker productivity raise the cost significantly. Arthritis self-management programs lower both costs and pain, with some programs reducing pain by 20 percent and visits to physicians by 40 percent. But fewer than 1 percent of patients have access to such programs.

- Sixty-four percent of Americans, or 130 million people, are overweight or obese in America today, increasing their risks for diabetes, heart disease, arthritis, and certain types of cancer. Even modest weight reduction can reduce these risks and their medical costs. Weight loss of just 8 percent has been shown to decrease the risk of diabetes by 55 percent. A loss of eleven pounds by a woman of average weight can reduce her risk of knee arthritis by 50 percent. Prevention of obesity could eliminate 14 percent of deaths from cancer in men and an even higher percentage in women. Medical costs due to overweight and obesity have accounted for one fourth of the rise in medical spending per person in recent years.

Imagine the progress we can make if we adopt a program that rewards best practices and encourages patients to follow them. The cost savings would be immense. There is no excuse for inaction.

The Problem of the Uninsured

Lack of health insurance in America is as certain a killer as diabetes or stroke. In fact, death due to lack of health insurance is the seventh-largest killer in the nation.

Some try to divert attention from this crisis by claiming that the uninsured can obtain adequate care in public hospitals. But these hospitals are designed to treat emergencies, not to provide long-term and comprehensive outpatient services. Those who wait for an emergency before they seek medical care often receive it too late. Even if it is not too late, the treatments available at this point are less likely to cure the problem or forestall it for long. The cost is high. Modern health care should not mean waiting until you have an emergency. It should prevent emergencies and improve the quality of life by detecting tumors while they can still be treated, ulcers before they burst, and heart problems before they cause heart attacks.

The facts are clear. Uninsured Americans are far less likely to be screened for cancer and other diseases. When they are finally diagnosed with a disease, it is usually at a significantly later stage than those who are insured. The Kaiser Family Foundation estimates that one third of the uninsured go without needed care, including 270,000 children with asthma. Thirty-two thousand Americans with heart disease go without bypass surgery or angioplasty because they are uninsured. Women with breast cancer are half as likely to receive treatment before their cancer has spread. Tens of thousands of Americans die needlessly each year due to lack of health insurance.

There are racial and ethnic dimensions to the crisis as well. Only one in ten white Americans is uninsured, but one in five African Americans, and one in three Hispanic Americans is uninsured. Surely we cannot continue to ignore these obvious disparities and injustices.

The Inadequacy of Employer-Based Coverage

Business is the main provider of private health insurance in the nation. More than 170 million people are insured through their employers. But the extent of this coverage has declined sharply in the past quarter century. In 1979, nearly 70 percent of employees had health insurance coverage. Today, only 55 percent do, and the coverage is still lower for women, African Americans, and Hispanic Americans.

Even when employees are insured, denial of coverage for so-called preexisting conditions, especially for mental health conditions, remains a problem. We have broadened the coverage with recent legislation, but there is still much to do. New drugs are often left out of coverage. Missing a week or two of work can cause employees to lose their jobs and their coverage. Applying for reimbursements is typically tedious and complex.

Serious illness can destroy people financially, and often does. A woman in her fifties from Toms River, New Jersey, went back to school after having children and earned a master's degree in social work at Fordham University. While employed as a social worker at a visiting nurse agency in 2003, she suffered a stroke after knee surgery and was left unable to speak, work, or care for herself. Her health insurance covered only a small part of her costs. She was left with twenty thousand dollars in unpaid medical bills, owed twenty-five thousand dollars in student loans for the degree, and had seven thousand dollars in credit card debt. Even though she had done everything right before her stroke—going back to college to obtain a master's degree, working hard in her chosen field, paying for health insurance, and paying off her student loans and credit card debt on time— she could no longer work and was forced into bankruptcy. Cases like hers are far too common in America today.

Citizens risk losing their livelihoods, their homes, and their financial security because of an illness or accident. As Dr. David Himmelstein of Harvard Medical School has said, "Unless you're Bill Gates you're just one serious illness away from bankruptcy. Most of the medically bankrupt were average Americans who happened to get sick."

One particularly ironic aspect of such tragedies is that those who have health insurance often lose their eligibility because an illness prevents them from returning to work. They are trapped in an impossible dilemma: They are insured only if they can work. If they get sick, they can lose their jobs and their insurance too. That has to change.

The Burden on Business

Our long-standing system of employer-based health insurance is sick as well, and recovery is far from certain. Ever-growing costs of care are making businesses more and more reluctant to offer coverage to employees. The burden on firms that do not provide it is putting them at an increasingly serious competitive disadvantage because of soaring costs. This problem is yet another price we pay for a health system that requires reform.

In 2005, General Motors launched a media campaign to bring attention to the high costs of health insurance. The company estimated that its employee health plan adds fifteen hundred dollars to the price of every new car. Ten percent of the cost of steel manufactured in the United States represents health benefits paid to retirees. Canada's national health care plan saves the Canadian auto industry four dollars an hour in employee benefits. The Canadian branches of the Big Three automobile manufacturers in the United States and the Canadian Auto Workers Union released a joint letter stating that their health care system is a "strategic advantage for Canada" and "has been an important ingredient" in the success of Canada's "most important export industry."

A study by President Clinton's chief economist, Laura D'Andrea Tyson, found that rising health costs were deterring job creation. If businesses were relieved of the cost of employee health insurance, her study found, our international competitiveness would be strengthened and businesses would hire more workers at better wages. Clearly, if health costs keep rising faster than inflation, our competitive position in the world will be weakened. Increased competition in today's global economy is an additional reason for easing the burden of health costs.

Costs of the Current System

The causes of the current problems are numerous. But some economists say that a major reason is the complexity and confusion inherent in how the wide array of health care services are now provided. Some propose leaving these problems to the marketplace, reducing regulation, and trusting competition to solve the crisis. But markets work best when products are straightforward and both businesses and consumers have enough information to make intelligent decisions. There is no evidence that costs have risen more slowly in the private health care industry than in government-operated programs like Medicare. To the contrary, the evidence proves just the opposite. Trusting competition to cure the problem is a pipe dream.

Medical services are rarely simple and their outcomes are often uncertain. It is far more difficult to compare the quality of one doctor's advice with another's than to compare the quality of cars, computers, mutual funds, or products in the supermarket. Free markets work well in the latter cases, though we must still keep high regulatory standards.

Health services are very different. Some doctors recommend expensive drugs and high-technology treatments. Others say we should avoid them. Some recommend intensive care or acute care; others are reluctant to do so when alternatives are available. It is also difficult to judge the quality of hospitals or medical clinics or mental health institutions. A further problem in health care decisions is that the consequences can be so grave—often a matter of life and death. The fact that health care costs can be large enough to cause financial ruin complicates these decisions.

Market inefficiencies also contribute to the high costs that cause so many Americans to be uninsured. A strong case can be made for federal financing to cover all individuals, along with federal rules and guidelines to promote best practices and the greatest efficiency. That was the solution Congress finally reached when it enacted Medicare in 1965 for senior citizens, and it has worked brilliantly ever since in covering doctors' and hospitals' bills for the elderly. The controversial reforms enacted in 2005 revolved solely around how to cover prescription drugs, which had not been an issue when Medicare was first enacted.

In fact, Medicare itself had been delayed a generation, until the 1960s, because of the intense political opposition of the American Medical Assocation, which felt it was "socialized medicine." President Roosevelt had originally considered including Medicare as part of Social Security in the 1930s, but the ideological debate derailed it. Few would argue now that Medicare was a mistake. And if the miracle of today's prescription drugs had been available in 1965, they would certainly have been included in Medicare, and the entire messy debate of recent years on prescription drugs under Medicare would have been avoided.

Obviously, our health care system as now structured is too costly. It is inefficient and does not adequately create incentives to provide the best care. It does not create effective competition among health providers or insurance companies. It is a highly fragmented industry, with thousands of insurance companies, hospitals, physicians, and other providers. It fails to make use of information technology, as a more centralized system would do. The lack of use of new technologies is costly and slows the adoption of the best practices. The political power of hospitals, health providers, and pharmaceutical companies also leads to higher costs. Ironically, America has fewer doctors and hospital beds per person than many other nations, but we spend more on them.

Administrative expenses are a large part of the problem. A single transaction in health care can cost the fragmented industry as much as twenty-five dollars. In contrast, banks have reduced their costs to less than a penny per transaction through modern information technology. Doctors' offices and hospitals are overwhelmed by the paperwork they have to complete in order to be reimbursed for medical procedures. Outdated administrative functions now cost $600 billion a year—dollars that could be far better spent on patient care.

A recent study found that administrative expenses and industry profits comprised 31 percent of total medical costs in 1999, or $1,059 per person. In Canada, where health care is delivered through a single-payer, government-run system, the same administrative expenses were 17 percent of total costs, or

$307 per person. For Medicare, the figure is even lower, 3 percent. No doubt, the Canadian system has drawbacks, but Canada spends far less on high-quality health care than we do. Medicare is far more efficient today in terms of administrative costs than our private health care system.

Because of the complexities of the current system, patients often cannot navigate their way through the large number of phone calls and authorizations needed to obtain the medical care they are paying for each week in their paychecks. At times when they are ill and most vulnerable, they often have to telephone for preauthorizations for medical procedures, and they inevitably end up receiving bills that they are not necessarily responsible for. They typically have little understanding of their insurance coverage, but who can blame them? The rules are excessively complicated for everyone.

In sum, for the vast amounts we spend, we have a health care system that is not performing well. It is too costly for too many, and large numbers of our citizens have no health insurance coverage at all. Coverage is often denied for specific or preexisting conditions. The system is highly inefficient because of its extreme fragmentation. It does not adequately encourage best practices or preventive medicine, and it is not truly competitive.

With medical advances becoming ever more expensive, the need for reform is all the greater. This new century is already producing more medical miracles than the system can absorb or afford. How can we ignore the need?

A Plan for the Health Care That America Deserves

I believe strongly that it is time for a new method of coverage financed by the federal government and available to all Americans, regardless of their age, their preexisting conditions, or their jobs. It will make bankruptcy caused by medical bills a thing of the past.

It will be a system that runs efficiently, draws on the newest information technologies, and drastically reduces administrative and marketing expenses. By covering all Americans, it will reduce the costs of public hospitals, which typically serve the poor, whose medical problems usually have reached the most expensive stages when they decide to seek treatment.

It will also be a system that rewards doctors and hospitals for adopting the best practices. Too often today's system encourages expensive high-technology treatments rather than needed prevention. Preventive programs do not reward health practitioners and hospitals, but a government program can do so fairly and fully.

The most effective option is to expand Medicare to cover all Americans. Since its enactment in 1965, Medicare has provided high-quality health care to hundreds of millions of Americans. It gives patients a clear guarantee that they will be able to see the doctor of their choice and it does not interfere with doctor-patient relationships. Largely because of Medicare, senior citizens enjoy a much higher quality of life and far greater economic security now than at any time in our history.

Medicare reflects the best of the American tradition of fundamental fairness and shared progress. Its administrative costs are low, because its marketing expenses are small and it has no highly paid executives. Its simple administrative structure keeps costs down and easily disseminates needed information on the practice of health care, including better use of information technology and better coordination of care.

We can improve Medicare as we expand it, to make it suitable for all Americans. Basic screening and testing for childhood diseases should be added, for example, as should greater coverage of preventive tests for adults. Promising initiatives should be expanded to reward high-quality care and improve the integration of services for patients with multiple diseases. The growing need for mental health services requires greater coverage for these conditions as well. We must also make certain that all patients benefit from secure, private electronic health records that enable their doctors to avoid errors, reduce costs, and improve care.

Such a plan will decouple health care from a person's job. Workers will have greater flexibility to change jobs. One of the most dreaded aspects of corporate layoffs, the loss of health insurance coverage, would be removed. Businesses would be relieved of the large costs they currently pay for health benefits.

The plan will cover everyone, provide substantial incentives to improve care, and result in significant savings. Electronic medical records could save $140 billion a year by improving quality and reducing duplicative care and administrative costs. The lower administrative costs of Medicare will result in major additional savings. Universal coverage itself will be cost-effective, because so many more Americans will obtain their care earlier and more effectively.

Since businesses will save so much as their employee health care obligations decline, it is fair to finance a large part of the plan through higher payroll taxes on both employers and employees, as well as from general tax revenues. Even with such an increase, employers and employees will still not be contributing as much of their budgets to health care as they do today. For society as a whole, the reduced expenditures will be significant, and we will be a healthier nation as well.

To ease the transition to the new system, the plan could be implemented in two stages; first for those between fifty-five and sixty-five and for children eighteen or younger. In the second phase, coverage would be extended to all other Americans not already covered by Medicare.

Universal health coverage would save Americans money and improve their health and their lives. For too long the nation has been AWOL in responding to these challenges. Health costs have been increasing far more rapidly than incomes and more and more citizens are left out of today's defective system.

My greatest hope is for an intense emphasis on preventive care, especially for children. The old saying that an ounce of prevention is worth a pound of cure is truer than ever. We have it within our power to correct these mounting problems. One of the proudest achievements of the early years of this new century should be to make affordable high-quality health care available to every member of every family of every community of every state in America. If we succeed, the lack of access to care will no longer claim lives or blight the days of those who cannot afford a doctor or a needed prescription. Illness will no longer bring financial ruin to any family. Businesses will no longer be hamstrung by ever-rising health costs they can't control and can't avoid. Improved and extended to all our people, Medicare will make the vast promise of this life-sciences century a reality for all Americans.

CHAPTER SIX

Continuing the March of Progress

Nothing has made me prouder as a U.S. senator for more than four decades than to participate in the expansion of civil and other rights to include all Americans. Intense and passionate battles have brought greater fairness to a society whose fundamental objective since the Declaration of Independence has been equal opportunity for all.

We have fought such battles repeatedly in our history. At our founding as a nation, not all were included in the original words of equality enshrined in the Constitution, especially women and people of color. The American story is one of men and women sacrificing their blood, sweat, and tears to give fuller meaning to the words that first gave life to our nation.

In the nineteenth century we fought a civil war to end the abhorrent practice of slavery. In the early 1900s we established new rights for workers and gave women the right to vote. In the 1930s, during the New Deal, we took major steps to protect the poor, the elderly, and the unemployed. We surely did not move fast enough, but we made continuing progress over time.

The modern phase of the battle for civil rights began in 1948, when President Harry Truman issued his famous executive order banning segregation in the armed forces. At the time, racial prejudice was widespread and undeniable, yet people hardly paid attention. African Americans were denied access to public places. Public schools were segregated, diminishing educational opportunity for African Americans. Neighborhoods were almost entirely divided along racial lines, often as the result of outright discrimination. African Americans were systematically denied the right to vote because of poll taxes, literacy requirements, and other measures.

The march of progress moved into high gear with the landmark Supreme Court decision in *Brown v. Board of Education* in 1954, which prohibited segregation in public schools. To me, this was another "shot heard 'round the world," a ringing restatement of America's greatness, a powerful declaration by the nation's highest court that separate could never be equal, that segregated schools meant unequal education and unequal opportunity for African Americans. We knew we could change that. We proceeded to integrate our public schools. We sought to make our entire American community work better, and we succeeded beyond all expectations.

In a dramatic four-year period in the 1960s we enacted three of the finest civil rights bills in our history. President Kennedy had proposed strong and far-reaching civil rights legislation before his death, and President Johnson steadfastly took up that battle. In the Civil Rights Act of 1964 we provided broad antidiscrimination protection in public places, in schools, and on the job for people of every color, ethnic background, or gender. In the Voting Rights Act of 1965 we guaranteed the right of African Americans to vote in America, and soon almost equal proportions of blacks and whites were registered to vote. In the Fair Housing Act of 1968 we out-lawed discrimination in housing and struck a powerful blow against segregation in our neighborhoods.

One of my own major early efforts as a senator was to abolish state poll taxes that were used to prevent African Americans from voting. The Twenty-fourth Amendment to the Constitution, adopted in 1964, had banned such taxes in federal elections, and a proposal I offered to the Voting Rights Act in 1965 would have banned them in state elections. We came within a few votes of victory in the Senate against this nefarious tax, which denied our most basic right to millions of Americans. A year later, the Supreme Court declared such taxes unconstitutional.

Subsequently, in 1970, when the Voting Rights Act was ex-tended by Congress, I offered a proposal to reduce the mini-mum age for voting from twenty-one to eighteen. It was included in the final bill, signed into law by President Nixon, and has opened new opportunities for young Americans to be part of the political process.

This march of progress was neither easy or inevitable. The courageous protests led by Martin Luther King, Jr., brought necessary attention to grave violations of civil rights. It was a tragically violent time that often pitted blacks against whites and men against women. It took a century after the abolition of slavery to win full democracy for African Americans, but we had achieved it at last. Women, too, and other minorities were protected from discrimination by federal legislation during this time. The march of progress was not to be stopped, at least not yet.

In recent decades, however, we have suffered setbacks. There have been court challenges to the laws that integrate public schools, that allow colleges to adopt affirmative action, that protect the disabled, and that guarantee women's access to college playing fields. After promising to leave the ban on discrimination against women untouched, the Bush administration proposed changes to weaken it. There have been shameful state efforts to adopt new laws that make it harder for African Americans to vote, and to gerrymander electoral districts to minimize the effectiveness of minority voting. Justice Department lawyers concluded in 2003 that a Texas law rearranging voting districts violated the Voting Rights Act, but they were overruled by political appointees in the department.

Government agencies created to monitor and enforce laws passed by Congress and reaffirmed by the courts have been undermined. The Occupational Safety and Health Administration, after being weakened significantly by President Reagan, was weakened still further under the current President Bush. The Equal Employment Opportunity Commission, created in 1964 to enforce antidiscrimination laws in the workforce, has been undermined, and recently the Bush administration has tried to weaken it still further.

We need to halt this deliberate reversal of progress and find the way to move forward again. There are more barriers to overcome. We have made great progress, and Americans are rightly proud of what we've accomplished. But we all know that people of color still face barriers to a good education and good jobs. Women are still paid less than men for the same work. Americans with disabilities still face obstacles to full participation in their communities. Gays and lesbians face discrimination, and

152

even violence rooted in bigotry. Workers are still denied their rightful voice in the workplace. Immigrants still face abuse. Civil rights and equal opportunity remain the great unfinished business of America.

Continuing the march of progress is not just a matter of fairness, or even simple justice. Our business and military leaders understand this basic principle. In a major Supreme Court case in 2003 challenging the University of Michigan's admissions policies, they came to the defense of affirmative action in higher education. In upholding some of the university's policies, the Court relied specifically on statements by the military such as this: "A highly qualified, racially diverse officer corps . . . is essential to the military's ability to fulfill its principal mission to provide national security." The Court also relied on this statement by the business community: "Skills needed in today's increasingly global marketplace can only be developed through exposure to widely diverse people, cultures, ideas and viewpoints." Our strength and progress—even our security—depend on it. We need the skills and contributions of everyone to meet today's challenges. Together we can build a brighter tomorrow.

Ending Racial Discrimination

Some claim that racial discrimination is dead in America. Not true. Racial equality has not yet been achieved. African Americans today, rather than becoming more optimistic after the progress of recent decades, are pessimistic that they will ever

153

achieve racial equality. Studies show that half of whites think we are close to achieving racial equality, but only one in five African Americans think we are. Even most whites know we haven't achieved equality yet. Only one in three believe we have. Only one in sixteen African Americans believe it.

One of my major concerns is that there is now widespread apathy on issues involving racial prejudice, in part because weak national leadership that has contributed to the stalling, and sometimes the reversal, of progress.

As Figure 6 (see page 157) makes clear, the typical African American man today makes only 75 percent of what white men earn. That is only a single percentage point higher than it was in the mid-1970s, after which the gap widened in the Reagan years, narrowed in the Clinton years, and has widened again under the Bush administration. Hispanic American men's earnings are lower now than they were in the 1970s, although this disparity is distorted by the influx of low-skilled immigrants. African American women also make significantly less than white women, although both groups have reduced the gap with men.

There has been some good news. If we compare members of racial groups who have the same education, the earnings gap has declined. African American men and women are now reaching the white-collar managerial class in larger numbers. But most of the progress has been in midlevel management and clerical tasks, not in the upper levels of management.

Most disturbing, the unemployment rate of African Americans remains consistently twice that of whites. Hispanic unemployment rates are higher still.

Some claim there are explanations other than prejudice for these differences. But there is no doubt that bigotry still poisons the workplace. In 2003 researchers at the University of Chicago and Harvard conducted an experiment. They sent résumés to numerous employers. Each résumé described a job applicant with almost identical qualifications, but in half the cases the names of the applicants were made to seem white, and in the other half, to seem African American. In every industry, the researchers found significant discrimination against those with seemingly African American names. Those applicants were

Year	White men	African American men	Hispanic American men	White women	African American women	Hispanic American women
1970	100	69.0	n.a.	58.7	48.2	n.a.
1975	100	74.3	72.1	57.5	55.4	49.3
1980	100	70.7	70.8	58.9	55.7	50.5
1985	100	69.7	68.0	63.0	57.1	52.1
1990	100	73.1	66.3	69.4	62.5	54.3
1992	100	72.6	63.3	70.0	64.0	55.4
1994	100	75.1	64.3	71.6	63.0	55.6
1995	100	75.9	63.3	71.2	64.2	53.4
1996	100	80.0	63.9	73.3	65.1	56.6
1997	100	75.1	61.4	71.9	62.6	53.9
1998	100	74.9	61.6	72.6	62.6	53.1
1999	100	80.6	61.6	71.6	65.0	52.1
2000	100	78.2	63.4	72.2	64.6	52.8
2003	100	78.2	63.3	75.6	65.4	54.3
2004	100	75.3	64.2	76.1	66.7	56.4

SOURCE: NATIONAL COMMITTEE ON PAY EQUITY

Figure 6. **Median Income by Race and Gender** (percentage)

called in for job interviews much less frequently than those with white-sounding names. Other studies support these findings.

Evidence of blatant discrimination in housing is also clear. Despite concerted efforts to desegregate housing, African Americans, whites, and Hispanic Americans still live separately in America. Some believe that this is merely a matter of choice. But discriminatory practices in housing and mortgage approvals are more subtle than they once were. Fewer banks compete to provide loans to minorities, which results in higher interest rates for them. When minorities express interest in buying a home, real estate agents often provide them with fewer choices.

Housing discrimination is harmful in several ways. Owning a home is the main source of wealth in America. The net worth for typical white families is ten times that for African American families, and the gap is growing. The economic plight of Hispanic American families compared to white households is dire as well. Minorities, whose home ownership is already lower than it is for whites, are often shut out of markets where growth in value is likely to be strongest. Housing discrimination also relegates minority children to neighborhoods with higher rates of crime, poorer health care, and inferior education. Since public schools are financed locally, schools that are predominantly African American or Hispanic American often lack good teachers, advanced curricula, adequate classrooms, and other resources and are less likely to be safe.

The 1960s began many years of reducing the education gap across America between minorities and whites, but the gap has begun to widen again. The proportion of minority students who graduate from high school now almost equals that of whites. But the proportion who go on to college is still low. Achievement levels measured by standardized tests narrowed between the 1960s and 1980s, but began to widen again in the 1990s.

A major reason is that America's schools, like its neighborhoods, suffer from de facto segregation. The battle against legal segregation of schools has been won. We fought bruising and bitter battles even in Massachusetts to end it. But the victory began to be reversed in the mid-1980s. Desegregation orders were terminated by state and appellate courts, and also by the Supreme Court. Today Hispanic Americans are segregated from other racial and ethnic groups, and they have the highest dropout and lowest graduation rates.

If we cannot equalize educational opportunities for these children, the American dream of equal opportunity becomes a sham. What can be done?

Our current educational system fails in two respects. Its quality lags behind that of other nations, and it is highly unequal. The burden is typically borne by minorities, and the nation often seems to be moving backward now, not forward. If the No Child Left Behind Act had been properly funded as promised by President Bush, we would have made real progress. But President Bush repeatedly failed to seek adequate funding, and Congress refused to provide it.

It is clear that we must have a larger role for the federal government in setting standards and equalizing funding of public schools throughout the nation. The evidence that an early start is imperative for doing well in school makes a strong system of early childhood education essential if we are to move forward in America.

Affirmative action, approved in a strong decision by the Supreme Court in 1978, has been repeatedly challenged in recent years. Study after study has demonstrated the benefits of racial diversity in college life. It creates new opportunities for minorities and broadens the perspectives of all students. William G. Bowen and Derek Bok, in their 1998 book, *The Shape of the River,* summarize convincingly how useful affirmative action has been. Among their most heartening findings is that so many young Americans of color, after graduating from selective schools, enter public life. We must continue to support this cornerstone of inclusiveness in modern America.

If we begin with improving and broadening education, however, we cannot end there. Two of the major government subsidies for home ownership are the tax deductions granted for mortgage interest and property taxes. But a sizable proportion of African Americans and Hispanics benefit less from the tax deductions because their incomes are low. We should give first-time home buyers a tax credit instead of a tax deduction for their mortgage interest and property taxes, since the subsidy would be larger. The tax credit should also be made refundable, so that lower-income taxpayers would receive it even if the taxes they owe are less than the full value of the credit. The additional benefit to low-income home buyers would be substantial. For taxpayers in the lowest tax bracket, each $1,000 in a tax deduction would save $100, while $1,000 in a tax credit would save the full $1,000—ten times more than a deduction. Those whose total taxes are less than $1,000 would receive a check from the government for the balance.

We must also make sure that those who are victims of discrimination have their day in court. Our current laws contain numerous protections against racial discrimination. But these laws must be fully enforced, and the courts have set back the march of progress for minorities in several key cases in recent years. Individuals have been barred from obtaining relief even though government practices have had a particularly adverse impact on minorities as a whole. It's difficult to obtain relief if school funding is unequal, or if toxic waste sites are disproportionately located in low-income neighborhoods. Job applicants are sometimes asked to waive their right to bring discrimination suits as a condition of employment. In each of these areas Congress has not been vigilant enough, and minorities have suffered.

Government contracts must include more minority-owned and women-owned businesses. The evidence of discrimination in the construction industries is widespread. The share of government contract dollars received by businesses owned by minorities or women is too low. Incredibly, the Bush administration suspended such programs in contracts for the reconstruction of areas devastated by Hurricane Katrina. This was exactly the wrong approach, and the action was quickly reversed because of the public outcry. But it was characteristic of an administration that neglects minorities and women on a regular basis.

We also have to be more effective in rooting out racial discrimination in our criminal justice system. The incarceration rate of minorities for nonviolent offenses is unconscionably high compared to the rate for whites. Equally unconscionable is the use of racial and ethnic profiling by law enforcement agencies against African Americans, Hispanic Americans, immigrants, Muslims, and Arab Americans.

There is too much injustice in our justice system. When persons are charged with crimes, it should not matter whether they are rich or poor, or male or female, or what their ethnic background is. One of the basic principles of our democracy is that when a person goes on trial for a crime, all that matters is guilt or innocence. But too often the system is biased against defendants for reasons that no fair system should tolerate. The abuse is most flagrant in capital cases, but many other defendants suffer unfairly as well.

When he served as attorney general, my brother Robert Kennedy said, "The poor man charged with crime has no lobby." We need look no further than Tulia, Texas, to know that those words still ring true today.

In 1999, more than 10 percent of Tulia's African American population was arrested in a supposed drug sting by a lone undercover narcotics officer. Most of the residents of this small Texas town caught up in the raid were African American. Some were Hispanic Americans, and a few were white. All of them were poor. Most of them were convicted and jailed—although the arrests produced no guns, no drugs, and no cash to support charges of illegal drug activity. The only evidence against many of the defendants was the word of the undercover agent who arrested them. At the time of the arrests he had been officially suspended for charges of theft and misconduct in a previous law enforcement position, but was still serving as an undercover officer.

As we know now, and as would have been obvious if those

arrested had received the fair trial and the effective legal representation guaranteed under the Constitution, the story of the Tulia drug ring was a pure fabrication. The accused were innocent of the crimes for which they were convicted. Yet a husband and father of two was sentenced to twenty years in prison. A fifty-seven-year-old farmer received a ninety-nine-year sentence. The term "miscarriage of justice" doesn't even begin to describe the wrongs committed here, and this tragic experience has been a constant nightmare for those wrongfully accused and their families.

But greater even than the devastating personal impact on the individual victims is the failure of the legal system. Where were the checks and balances that could have prevented these convictions? Why did juries time and again convict the defendants on such flimsy evidence? How could a judge allow it? What happened to the right to a fair trial and the right to effective assistance of counsel?

Our multibillion-dollar correctional system often isn't correcting anything. The United States now locks away more than 2 million people in its prisons and jails. One and a half million children have a parent behind bars. Some 630,000 inmates are released from prison each year—1,700 every day. Within three years 63 percent will be rearrested for a felony or a serious misdemeanor.

No one can look at these data and say that current policies on incarceration are working. The criminal justice system is failing all of us, at enormous cost to public safety and to the integrity of families and communities. It is time to accept the fact that we cannot jail our way to safety.

To break the vicious cycle of crime, punishment, and recidivism we need major reforms at both the state and the federal level. We need to revise or even eliminate mandatory minimum sentences because they too often prevent the punishment from fitting the crime. We need to stop prisons from becoming breeding grounds for crime, a goal that can be accomplished by improving security, offering effective support for prison education, and providing help for prisoners with mental illnesses.

We also need coordinated efforts by law enforcement agencies and community groups to give prisoners a helping hand after their release. The vast majority of them will use that help to become productive members of the community. We know that these reforms will light the way to a fairer and safer future. The question is whether elected officials are wise enough to reject partisan appeals and "lock-'em-up" sound bites long enough to see that light.

Ending Discrimination Against Women, Gays, and the Disabled

When both spouses in a family work, our economy places an unfair burden on women. Most often, they are the ones who bear the greatest burden in balancing care for the family and their responsibilities at work. Discrimination against women continues in America. On average, they still earn 25 percent less than men. In most fields, even when they do the same work, they earn less than men. Male kindergarten teachers, for example, earn five thousand dollars more a year on average than female kindergarten teachers.

Over time, the pay gap becomes even greater because women often must leave their job to care for their family. They lose their wages, and they lose opportunities for promotion. One study found that over a fifteen-year period, a typical working woman earns less than 40 percent of what a typical man earns. Women endure further burdens in retirement. They are less likely to have pensions, and the pensions they do have pay less. Gender discrimination also keeps well-qualified women from pursuing the careers they want. In fact, women comprise 90 percent of those who work full-time and earn fifteen thousand a year or less. One of the most important reforms we can accomplish is to require public disclosure of information about pay.

In 1993, after a long battle, Congress enacted the Family and Medical Leave Act, which guarantees twelve weeks of unpaid leave a year for millions of workingmen and -women to care for themselves, their newborn or newly adopted children, or family members facing serious illness.

This protection is especially important for women. Since its passage, more than 50 million Americans have been able to take job-protected time off when they need it most. Twenty-six million Americans have used the leave to care for their own serious illness, 15 million have taken it to care for a family member, and 9 million have taken it to care for a new child.

Some had argued that businesses could not afford such leave for their employees, but the doomsayers were wrong. A report by the Department of Labor showed that the law has had either a positive or neutral effect on profitability in 90 percent of businesses and a positive or neutral effect on productivity in 84 percent of businesses.

The law is not always satisfactory, however, since many employees decline to use the leave for fear of losing their job or losing their paycheck.

Under current law, the leave is unpaid. Some states have acted to end that injustice, but the vast majority have not. In addition, the law applies only to companies with fifty or more employees. We should reduce that number to twenty-five, to make the leave available to more employees.

A further worthwhile reform would be a federal guarantee of seven paid days of sick leave a year, a step that would benefit 66 million Americans. Guaranteeing paid sick days is a matter of basic decency, but it is also vital for public health. Too often employees come to work sick and infect coworkers and customers. This issue is a particular concern of the food services industry, where 86 percent of workers who cook or serve food in restaurants and cafeterias across the nation every day do not have paid days of sick leave.

A court ruled recently that because of the lack of such leave, a stomach virus in one worker infected six hundred guests and three hundred employees at the Reno Hilton Hotel in Nevada.

Paid sick days can actually save businesses money through reduced turnover and increased productivity. A recent study at Cornell University found that sick workers on the job cost businesses $180 billion annually in lost productivity. Improving current law would give greater peace of mind to employees, and businesses would save $8 billion a year from reduced turnover and increased productivity in their workforce.

To reduce discrimination against women, Congress made a historic national commitment in 1972 to give our daughters the same opportunities in higher education as our sons. This commitment, known as Title IX of the 1972 law, isn't only for sports, although sports receive most of the attention because the change there has been so dramatic and successful. More and more women are studying at the highest levels in universities in a wide variety of fields. Nevertheless, more needs to be done. Gender discrimination still exists in schools and colleges. According to the National Coalition for Women and Girls in Education, young women and girls are underrepresented in many fields of study, such as engineering and the physical sciences, and female students are often guided toward fields considered to be "for women."

That's why it's so alarming that the Bush administration has sought to undermine this guarantee of equal access by women to the benefits of education. In the name of "flexibility" the administration has sought to weaken the ability of girls and women to challenge discrimination and continue our progress. We cannot allow this to happen.

In yet another major area—equal treatment of the disabled—the battle has been long, complex, and highly gratifying. Again and again we have acted to grant basic rights to disabled Americans, beginning with World War II veterans and eventually covering all persons with disabilities, including children. We improved the lives of both those with physical disabilities and those with mental disabilities, and of children with learning disabilities. We enabled voters with disabilities to get to the polls, and gave all persons with disabilities greater access to cultural and recreational activities in their communities. We required fair housing for people with disabilities and fair access to air travel. In 1990, the landmark Americans with Disabilities Act opened the doors wide by promising every disabled citizen a new and better life, and it is now the most important of all the civil rights laws for persons with disabilities.

This aspect of the civil rights revolution has been a bright star in our democracy. Open debate and direct participation of people with disabilities powerfully influenced these decisions. The legislation became ever more inclusive. For example, before 1975 four million disabled students received no help in school. Today, more than six million disabled children have access to public education.

The battle is not over, however. There have been serious legal challenges to the constitutionality of these laws, but so far the courts have upheld them, as they should. But the Supreme Court is closely divided on the issue, and newly appointed justices could alter the balance and reverse the progress we have made.

In recent years another important aspect of discrimination has become a pressing national issue. There should be no place in America for bias against persons because of their sexual preference. Yet evidence abounds that gays and lesbians are frequent victims of discrimination and even violence because of their sexual orientation.

Consider two examples. Kendall Hamilton of Oklahoma City, after working at Red Lobster for several years and receiving excellent employment reviews, applied for a promotion on the advice of his general manager. The manager knew he was gay, but a coworker informed upper management of his sexual orientation, and a person with far less experience was hired for the job. Hamilton was told his sexual orientation "was not compatible with Red Lobster's belief in family values."

Steve Morrison, a firefighter in Oregon, became the victim of hate mail and other harassment when coworkers saw him at a gay rights event on the TV news. After a lengthy administrative hearing, trumped-up charges against him were dismissed, but he had to be transferred to another fire station.

In America, this should not happen, and our people do not want it to happen. According to a 2003 Gallup poll, 88 percent of Americans believe that gays and lesbians should have equal job opportunities. That is the American way. More than 60 percent of Fortune 500 companies have adopted nondiscrimination policies to prevent such bigotry.

We cannot leave the task of dealing with these problems to the states or private industry, as some urge. In the Senate we've developed a strong bill to protect against sexual discrimination at work, and I'm disheartened that we have not yet been able to enact it.

We must also resist efforts by the president and some in Congress to prohibit gay marriage in America. To do so would be an unacceptable invasion of individual privacy. It reflects a politics of bigotry that is contrary to our values. Leadership in America must support tolerance and understanding. Inciting anger and retribution is the worst sort of wedge politics.

A serious related problem is that hate crimes in America are on the rise. These are crimes committed because of the victim's race, sexual orientation, gender, or disability. Twenty-five such crimes occur every day in America, and many more go unreported. We've made progress in passing strong federal laws against such crimes, especially against people of color and women. But we need to do more to strengthen them, particularly by including hate crimes against gays and lesbians.

Such crimes are an attack not just on individual victims but on whole communities. We must say loud and clear that those who commit such vicious crimes will go to prison.

In all of these areas we need a new overarching law to assure all Americans their day in court if they face discrimination. Too often in recent times, hard-won rights have been lost because of narrow judicial interpretations or because Congress has been less than clear in writing existing laws.

We need a new "fairness act" to correct these problems. Such a law would make it easier for victims of any form of discrimination to enforce their basic rights and obtain relief for violations. Many of the solutions may seem technical, but they mean the difference between dignity and discrimination, employment and unemployment, opportunity and poverty, the American dream and an American nightmare for millions of our fellow citizens.

Resuming the War Against Hunger and Poverty in America

It's a scandal and unacceptable that in this, the richest nation in the history of the world, millions of our fellow citizens go hungry night and day. It's equally unbelievable that one in six children in America lives in poverty. But sadly, hunger and poverty are alive and well in our society today.

According to the Department of Agriculture, more than 38 million Americans live in hunger. A report in December 2005 by the U.S. Conference of Mayors found that demands for emergency food assistance rose 12 percent over the preceding year, and that cities are unable to meet the need.

The number of persons living in hunger has gone up every year for the last five years, and it is higher today than ever before. No other industrial nation in the world has hunger on this scale.

More than one in three of those hungry are children, and their plight seriously impairs their ability to concentrate in school. It also leads to a chronic absences, illnesses, and behavioral problems. For adults, it is the harbinger of serious medical problems and hospitalization. As scientists have found, even mild hunger can result in serious malnutrition.

Hunger in America is also expensive, costing the nation billions of dollars a year in higher health costs and lost productivity. Charities cannot solve the problem; they have not been able to eliminate hunger in any nation.

It would cost us $12 billion a year to eliminate hunger. In fact, we could quickly eliminate hunger in a year, by expanding the successful food-stamp program and broadening the child nutrition programs we already have. Today, only two thirds of those who are hungry qualify for food stamps. We should also extend the reach of our nutrition programs for the elderly. We do not need a new bureaucracy. We need only to do more of what now works well. It is time for the march of progress in America to include the hungry as well.

Like hunger, child poverty is a scar on the American face of prosperity. Depending on how it is measured, we have the highest or second highest child poverty rate in the developed world, according to a comprehensive study headed by researchers at Syracuse University. Thirteen million children in America live in poverty—18 percent of all children, 33 percent for African American children, and 28 percent for Hispanic American children. Countries like Denmark and Finland have a child poverty rate of less than 3 percent.

Poor children deserve a decent opportunity for a full life, and we should make a clear commitment to provide it. In the 1930s, we made a similar commitment to the nation's elderly, and we succeeded. Poverty rates among the elderly are now low because of Social Security and Medicare. We need a similar commitment to children. Poor children are malnourished and have weaker immune systems. Lack of vital nutrition affects their learning abilities and makes them vulnerable to serious illness.

Often they are not ready for school at five or six. Unlike other children, they often cannot count and do not know their letters. Their lack of learning ability, if not improved early in life, usually means a permanent disadvantage.

Investing in poor children is one of the best investments the nation can make. It is repaid many times over in better workers, fewer social needs, and lower crime rates.

Even the most hard-hearted would agree that child poverty is no fault of the children. We can no longer afford to compete in the world when we waste these young resources. A realistic goal could cut the proportion of poor children in half over the next ten years, and I have proposed legislation to achieve it. It can be done. We did it for the elderly. We did it in the War on Poverty. When President Johnson proposed his antipoverty program, the poverty rate was nearly 20 percent, and it fell to below 12 percent. Great Britain has recently implemented an effective new program to reduce child poverty and America should do the same.

Protecting Our Heritage as a Nation of Immigrants

Finally, in the march of progress, immigrants deserve our commitment as well. In my family, we were vividly aware of the immigrant stories of our great-grandparents. All found the American dream, and I have been one of its fortunate beneficiaries.

Today, however, our immigration system is broken. We must reform it to reflect our values of family unity, economic opportunity, and fundamental fairness. Ten million illegal immigrants live in America today. But strong law enforcement alone is not the answer. We tripled the number of border patrol agents and quintupled the enforcement budget in 2004, but the number of illegal workers still increased.

The Center for American Progress estimates that apprehending and deporting the millions who are here illegally would cost more than $200 billion over the next five years, or more than $40 billion a year. Even if we could afford to take such action, we wouldn't do so because so many of them have become an indispensable part of the economy of communities in all parts of the country. The fact is, we need immigrants in America. Some sectors of our economy are heavily dependent on the contributions of immigrants. They comprise four out of ten jobs in farming, fishing, and forestry; three out of ten in building and ground maintenance; and two out of ten in food preparation and construction. Many of them are here illegally, but as business leaders agree, deporting them would cause massive disruptions in the economy.

Americans don't want borders locked shut or wide open. They want smart borders. We must bring illegal immigrants out of the shadows. In doing so we would also enable law enforcement to focus more intensively on terrorists and violent criminals.

Senator John McCain and I have sponsored legislation to deal effectively with these issues. We propose to create a new temporary visa that enables foreign workers to enter the country and fill available jobs that require their skills.

We also believe it is necessary to protect illegal workers already here. They will be given the opportunity to apply for the new visas and to enter the legal pipeline for a green card. They will be able to obtain medical treatment when needed. We also propose better law enforcement and more effective border patrols for the future.

In this age of terrorism we must obviously be vigilant about our immigration policy. But we can strengthen our security without weakening our proud heritage as a nation of immigrants. We cannot allow immigrants, especially Arabs and Muslims, to be rounded up based on their national origin or religion rather than on a specific assessment of whether they pose a threat. In the march of progress, this is one of the new frontiers we face, and it is essential for us to get it right, for our economy, for our heritage, and for our values.

From the time America won its independence, our nation has always been a work in progress. Its commitment to equality for all was a goal to which we aspired, and the Constitution created a firm foundation on which to reach it. Over the years we have learned how much there is to do, and we know today how much still remains to be accomplished. We also know that the march of progress must go on, or America will not be America.

CHAPTER SEVEN

Uniting America

ew things concern me more than the bitter divisions in
our society today. At our best as a nation we have faith
that our government is working toward common goals.
Those goals are clear. Government is the guarantor of the individual rights and equality for which our revolutionary heroes
fought. We claimed our freedom from a closed, repressive society and created a representative and open government to maintain that freedom. We were not perfect then, and the battle to
achieve our ideals remains unfinished. But our progress toward
including our entire community in our goals has been unmistakable. We have guaranteed greater rights and greater opportunities to more and more Americans over time. Our pursuit of
the goals of freedom and equality for all our people has been an
example to the world for more than two centuries.

But this spirit of community has been dimishished in the
past quarter century. A determined assault on government began under President Reagan. As it took hold and grew stronger,
government was wrongly characterized as favoring some of us
over all of us. It was seen as the chief cause of the economy's
problems, from stagnating wages and high unemployment to
inflation, poverty, the rising cost of health care, and the poor

quality of education. Social programs were not viewed as part of the struggle for the rights of all, but as a giveaway to some at the expense of the rest.

Candidates were elected to office who sought to reduce the size and scope of government indiscriminately, not to make it better. Appointees who had little or no experience in government or faith in its role were put in control of key departments and agencies. Many of these officials were dedicated only to reducing the size of their departments and relinquishing their power to enforce the laws they were appointed to uphold. As a result, government became less competent, not more competent.

In some areas, of course, government regulation *was* excessive, when competition could better serve the people and the nation. I myself was an early advocate of deregulation in areas where competition could better serve the public and the nation.

I believe in free enterprise, but rules are necessary to keep it free. Our antitrust laws are a vital part of maintaining competition, and government regulation is equally vital in preserving health and safety in the workplace. As Harvard Law School declares when awarding degrees to its graduating students, our laws are "Those wise restraints that make us free." In the 1970s I led the battle to free the airlines from cumbersome economic government regulation. I have enormous faith in our businesses and our entrepreneurs. Government has always been a vital partner in our economy as well. But the blunderbuss demands of the right wing that we downsize all areas of government ignore two hundred years of history—two hundred years of partnerships between business and government that made America the largest and most productive economy in the world.

We need to remind ourselves of this history. Early state governments built the revolutionary new canals. The first of these, the Erie Canal, opened in 1825 and soon made New York City the center of American commerce by opening trade to the growing West. Following this lead, the federal government began to build the new roads needed for national development. It also made public lands available at low prices to a nation of farmers and immigrants. The widening opportunity to own property in turn gave our people great confidence in their democracy.

By the 1830s, local governments were developing the free, mandatory public schools that would prepare the nation for both a representative government of informed citizens and a commercial society of able workers. Later in that century, the federal government subsidized railroads and invested in the new agricultural and technical colleges.

In the Progressive Era government's role broadened when it challenged the robber barons and set limits on concentrations of economic power. In the early 1900s we established minimum safeguards for workers and consumers. We adopted a progressive income tax on our citizens, and women won the right to vote. Government built the sewage and sanitation systems that made the new commercial metropolises possible. We established the Federal Reserve as the nation's central bank, to make the economy financially stable. State and local governments built high schools and guaranteed a "free and appropriate" public education for all citizens so that a well-trained and well-educated workforce would be available to meet the growing needs of business.

During the devastating Depression of the 1930s, unemployment rose above 25 percent and the nation lost a third of its income. In those years we redefined government's responsibility for the nation's economic well-being in a new social contract that protected citizens in times of adversity. We created Social Security and unemployment insurance. We strengthened the banking system and began regulating the securities markets. We established a minimum wage. We recognized that government was essential to stability, prosperity, and growth.

In the wake of World War II America fully accepted government's central role in the economy. The G.I. Bill of Rights enabled millions of veterans to go to college. The federal government undertook the building of the interstate highway system. It funded the great research facilities of the National Institutes of Health and made sure, through oversight by the FDA, that drugs were safe and effective. We sent men to the moon. Government research contributed vitally to the scientific discoveries that have helped all our people.

Many of these initiatives were priorities of President Kennedy's New Frontier and President Johnson's Great Society. In the 1960s the nation lifted up those trapped in a harsh underclass. Strong civil rights laws removed legal obstacles for our citizens, and the War on Poverty broke down barriers for the intractably poor. Medicare and Medicaid were created to provide decent health care for the elderly and the poor. Education was generously funded.

The evidence speaks for itself. During the twentieth century generations of low-wage employees, immigrants, and subsistence farmers found the key to the American dream of a decent wage, adequate health care, and a retirement immune from poverty. The American middle class was born during this century of social progress, and it thrived.

These achievements did not mean that government did not make mistakes. It happens in the private sector, too. Entrepreneurs create new businesses but also go bankrupt. Speculative markets rise rapidly, but they can also fall precipitously, leading to financial losses and damaging instability. Just as we allow businesses their mistakes so that they continue to take the risks that can blossom into successes, we must allow government its occasional mistakes in order to benefit from its many achievements. We strive to make both the private sector and the public sector work better and work together.

Some so-called experts claim that government spending is bad for business and bad for the economy, but good economic research tells us the opposite. Distinguished economists have documented the contributions that government can make to economic growth and standards of living. The conventional wisdom that large government and high taxes are harmful to rapid growth does not withstand careful and objective scrutiny.

Our own recent history has taught us an important lesson. I was in the Senate one day in 1993 when Texas senator Phil Gramm began to speak. He warned us that President Clinton's tax bill, which raised tax rates for upper income Americans, would undoubtedly cause the worst recession since the Great Depression. The unemployed would circle the Capitol, he predicted, and march up the steps of the Senate. He was wrong. Under President Clinton we created 22 million jobs, capital investment rose, and notwithstanding the higher taxes, the rich grew much richer.

In recent years, many have quoted President Kennedy about cutting taxes. The president advocated a tax cut that was eventually signed under President Johnson. What few recall is that at the time of President Kennedy's inauguration, the top tax bracket was 91 percent. Even with President Kennedy's cuts, tax rates were much higher then than they are today, yet the economy grew rapidly during that period. Government social programs were expanded in those years, and tens of millions of Americans found the key to the middle class for the first time.

One thing we know about our capitalist system. If one of us does well, it usually means others benefit, too, because Congress has sandpapered the system's rough edges. Government social programs and economic justice are compatible with rapid economic growth, and they also make vital contributions to it by maximizing the energies and talents of all Americans, not just some Americans.

Ending the Distrust of Government

Public opinion surveys tell us that Americans are now deeply skeptical of their leaders. "Politicians are all alike," they seem to be saying, "and we do not trust any of you." Two thirds of Americans disapprove of both the president and Congress. A large majority think the nation is headed in the wrong direction.

A nation so skeptical of its government and its other institutions is inevitably impaired. It cannot visualize its challenges clearly or take adequate action to respond to them. As hostility grows, it becomes a rot that saps our energy and creativity. It naturally seeks scapegoats and is easily exploited by opportunists. Those who perpetuate personal attacks and divisiveness in America are doing the nation a huge disservice.

The colossal failure of FEMA to manage the crisis caused by Hurricane Katrina in 2005 was a consequence of this assault on government. The hurricane did not catch the nation by surprise. Evacuations of New Orleans and surrounding areas were ordered when weather professionals predicted the storm could be one of the worst on record.

As the tragic damage mounted and the levees broke, FEMA reacted slowly, even casually. The effort was headed by a man with no experience in managing emergencies and no experience managing an organization of comparable size. He was known to the president through friends.

In addition to the ineptitude of men and women in high office, an attitude that government should wait and see, not act and anticipate, pervades this administration. In a time when terrorists might readily strike a bridge, a tunnel, or a levee, this laxness is a dangerous failure.

The nation also learned how insensitive its government had become toward the poor of the Gulf region. They were left to fend desperately for themselves while the middle class escaped by automobile.

I traveled to New Orleans a few weeks after the disaster. The water in the streets was as dark as ink. The filth, the waste, and the destruction were deplorable, and the poor were mired in it. Many lost everything, despite their best efforts.

Commentators who have made a career of putting down government tried to use the tragedy as a platform for their agenda. This was not a failure of those who ran the agency or the leadership in Washington, they said—it was a failure inherent in government. But the nation knew better. It was government that made Social Security one of the most effective institutions of any kind in any nation. It was government that made the National Institutes of Health a model of superb research. It was government that built the nation's highways. It was government that made it possible for millions of young men and women to go to college. It was government that conducted the research that led to the Internet revolution.

FEMA is not the only neglected agency in Washington. In 2005 more agencies were run by temporary acting heads than at any time in my memory. Many of those in positions of responsibility had no adequate background for the job. Even more disturbing has been the politicization of some of these agencies and departments. The Food and Drug Administration is supposed to approve prescription drugs based on careful scientific research. But a bipartisan congressional investigation found that the agency had decided to reject the so-called morning-after pill in the fall of 2005 before the scientific evidence was even presented. Clearly, the FDA must be an independent agency that makes decisions based on the best evidence, free from ideological or industry pressures.

A partisan political poison has infected voting rights as Republican officials at all levels of government and their allies attempt to reduce minority voting power. Few doubt that if voting in Florida had been fair in 2000, President Bush would not have been elected, and we would have a very different nation and world today.

The misuse and abuse of government power have undermined the rule of law and the nation's reputation in the world. Each new example or indictment demonstrates the arrogance of the administration and its culture of corruption. Too many men and women appointed to office seem to believe that government exists for their personal gain, not to serve the public.

Experienced and forthright officials who speak in honest disagreement with administration policies are attacked viciously and vindictively. As said in Chapter One, when General Eric Shinseki, the army chief of staff, insisted we would need more troops than the administration wanted to send to Iraq, he was forced out of the army he loved, well before his retirement age. When State Department official Richard Clarke criticized the Bush administration for ignoring Al Qaeda before September 11, the administration vilified him. When distinguished former diplomat and expert on Africa Joseph Wilson asserted that Iraq was not seeking uranium from Niger, as the administration claimed in making its case for war, officials retaliated by revealing to the press that Wilson's wife, Valerie Plame, was an undercover agent of the CIA. When UN arms inspector Hans Blix insisted on the eve of the war that he had found no weapons of mass destruction in Iraq, he became the target of administration criticism. When the head of the International Atomic Energy Agency, Mohamed ElBaradei, disagreed with administration claims, they tried to prevent him from serving a third term at the agency. He later won the Nobel Peace Prize.

The purpose of these vendettas was to chill open and public

discussion of major issues and stifle internal disagreements within the most important agencies in Washington. A functioning democracy depends on free and honest debate, but we have an administration today that has lost its way.

A Way to Unite Us

At times we may need less government; sometimes we may need more. But what we always need is a commitment to government that is both honest and competent.

To restore faith in government, it must be led by people who themselves understand and have faith in the public purpose. We cannot tolerate a government bent on undermining the integrity and competence of our finest institutions.

We can revive the unifying spirit of our American community by making government work again, and by holding it accountable for its actions when it departs from the nation's most important principles.

How can we unify the nation today? Thomas Jefferson's first inaugural address, in 1801, provides a source of inspiration. His eloquence was inspiring not only because of his talent for language, but also because he spoke from an unshakable belief in the nation's ideals. He had a soft and low-key voice, and Congress that day in March 1801 could hardly hear him. But his words spoke loudly to an angry and conflicted young nation: "Every difference of opinion is not a difference of principle. We have called by different names brethren of the same principle."

Those were very contentious times. Jefferson, the leader of

his party, was often contemptuous of his opponents, led by President John Adams. He feared what he thought were their monarchical tendencies. His fears were exaggerated, but in the process he helped establish the nation's devotion to individual rights.

Anger boiled over in the politics of the late 1790s, perhaps even more so than it does today. Jefferson is by no means above criticism, and Adams, his political rival, made vital and admirable contributions to the checks and balances on abuses of power. But Jefferson was our nation's first presidential optimist. For him, the idea of America was too powerful to fail. The new American government would protect individual rights, not usurp them, and would guarantee equal opportunity, rather than protect the rich and advantaged. I believe America must not only tolerate different opinions, but welcome and even encourage them. As Jefferson said, we are all brethren when it comes to our deepest principles, and by far the most effective way to apply them is through open and honest debate.

Today we have been diverted from this mission. Differences of opinion have been exploited for cynical political gain. But I believe our common allegiance to our Jeffersonian heritage is unshakable. It has held us together through times of massive crisis.

Not least of these was the Civil War. When the nation was torn by tragic divisions over slavery, Lincoln sought to unify America by restoring Jefferson's principles of liberty and equality as the foundation of the nation's beliefs. Lincoln's eloquence was matched in our history only by Jefferson's. We are, as Lincoln reminded us, a nation "dedicated to the proposition that all men are created equal."

An experience I had in the 1990s with the courageous first president of the Czech Republic, Václav Havel, has stayed with me. During the term of the first President Bush, Havel visited Washington as president of his nation newly freed after decades of repression under Nazi Germany and then the Soviet Union. I was fortunate to have an opportunity to spend some time with him during his visit, and I thought he'd like to see one of the most moving sites in our capital, the Lincoln Memorial.

When we arrived there, his aide began translating into Czech the famous words from Lincoln's Gettysburg Address and his second inaugural address engraved on the walls. Then Havel asked me to read Lincoln's words aloud. Havel was also one of his nation's leading authors and poets, and as he listened to the words as Americans hear them, I could see his eyes light up. He understood the power of a great leader's stirring appeal to a nation deeply in need of healing. Lincoln's words were poetry, and he was riveted by them.

Those words still have meaning for the life of every American. As Havel poignantly reminded me, liberty is the beacon of light that America sends around the earth. The world admires us for our commitment to liberty and equality above all else. The words of Lincoln ring everywhere. To the world, the American story is valiant and idealistic. We rid ourselves of tyranny more than two centuries ago and united our nation around the principles of freedom and equality. We fought twice in the twentieth century to free Europe on the basis of such principles.

Jefferson said in 1787 that America would need a rebellion every twenty years. What he meant was that our ideals have to be revitalized for each generation. Some would subordinate those ideals to other needs. Others would claim there are even higher principles. Still others simply forget them. We need that kind of rebellion now, to revive the nation's confidence in its deepest ideals. I have never believed, for all of today's divisiveness, that we are a permanently divided nation. But to regain our unity, we in government must keep the promise of liberty and equality.

Where do we begin?

The first step is to end the personal attacks. Character assassination is now a full-fledged occupation in politics. We have always prided ourselves on our pluralism. We are a diverse society and open to fair discourse about our disputes and disagreements. But we cannot accept a politics that makes bitter personal enemies of those who disagree and casts harsh aspersions on the morality and character of our opponents.

Politics was not always like this, not that it was ever all goodwill and flowers. In 1962 I had a difficult primary battle with a good man, Eddie McCormack, to win the Democratic nomination to be senator from Massachusetts. Eddie was well known in our state, and extremely able. He was the nephew of the Speaker of the House of Representatives John McCormack. Eddie and I fought a hard campaign, but we remained respectful friends. Eddie died in 1997, and I was honored to be asked to speak at his funeral.

In the general election in 1962 I defeated George Cabot Lodge, the Republican candidate. The Cabots and the Lodges had been involved in American politics since the earliest years of the Republic. My grandfather John Fitzgerald, both as a congressman and mayor, had long wrangled with George's great-grandfather Henry Cabot Lodge, Sr., the powerful senator who was often in political combat with President Woodrow Wilson. Grampa lost to Lodge in his campaign for the Senate in 1916. A generation later my brother Jack defeated George's father, Henry Cabot Lodge, Jr., for a Senate seat in 1952. It was an honest and fairly fought competition, and the families remained friendly. When I defeated George for the Senate in 1962, the friendship was not breached. George is a highly regarded professor emeritus of Harvard and was one of our most dedicated and able board members at the John F. Kennedy Institute of Politics there.

More recently, I fought a difficult battle with Republican Mitt Romney for the Senate in 2000. Mitt is a diligent Republican governor today in Massachusetts. We disagree on many matters, but we often work together for what we feel is the common good.

Such stories once were common. Adams and Jefferson were political antagonists who remained friends out of mutual respect for their common principles, and they left us one of the richest correspondences of our early history.

But there are too few stories like that in Washington and around the country today. The most pernicious personal attacks of recent years are the accusations of unpatriotic behavior when a senator or congressman criticizes the nation's war effort. What is truly unpatriotic is the attempt to shut down public debate about the Iraq war through such harsh accusations.

Military heroes like Max Cleland, John Kerry, John Murtha, and John McCain have been subjected to recent scurrilous attacks, often questioning their patriotism.

The exploitation of divisive wedge issues has run amok in American politics. Political specialists study how to frame issues in order to inflame passions. One example that is particularly personal for me and my family is religious freedom. Religious prejudice was part of the air we breathed as descendants of Irish immigrants. The overwhelming defeat of Al Smith by Herbert Hoover in the presidential election of 1928 was part of our common heritage. Smith, the spirited Irish governor of New York, was subjected to the vile anti-Catholicism so prevalent at the time, and that same bigotry was the single greatest challenge my brother faced in his campaign for president in 1960.

My family is very religious. But we are also dedicated to the principle of government neutrality on religion. Nothing else would better protect our right to worship as we choose and still participate fully in American life, public or private. After Al Smith's defeat, many believed a Catholic could not win the nation's highest office. But my brother made it scrupulously clear that his religious views would never influence his political decisions. That principle was at the heart of the American way, and he argued for it with great conviction.

As he told the Greater Houston Ministerial Association in September 1960, "I believe in an America where the separation of church and state is absolute. . . . I do not speak for my Church on public matters—and the Church does not speak for me."

If that basic principle is violated, he said, anyone could be a victim. He pointed out that it was Virginia's harassment of Baptist preachers that had led to Jefferson's famous statute of religious freedom.

He responded similarly as president in 1962, when the Supreme Court ruled that prayer in public schools was a violation of the Constitution. In defending the decision and successfully blunting the outcry against it at the time, he called it "a welcome reminder to every American family that we can pray a good deal more at home, we can attend our churches with a good deal more fidelity, and we can make the true meaning of prayer much more important in the lives of all of our children."

His firm belief in religious freedom was a victory for the protection of the religious rights of all Americans. It is especially hurtful that this basic principle is being undermined today by President Bush's proposals to use faith-based organizations to provide social services funded by the federal government. It crosses a boundary by potentially requiring people to practice or abide by religious principles in which they do not believe in order to receive necessary aid. This is not religious neutrality, and it is highly divisive in our modern society.

Intolerable, ugly innuendo about political opponents has also become rampant. Such behavior creates a vicious circle. Candidates respond in kind because they believe they have no other choice. Instead, we must debate openly and in good conscience about how to solve our problems. We must give the people every opportunity to hear opposing views, understand complex issues, and demand honest answers.

We must also be sure that candidates address the issues

important to their constituencies, not just to their wealthiest supporters. The personalization of politics has weakened this discourse and undermined the public response essential for effective government.

We cannot readily discuss issues like abortion, gay marriage, gun control, or even the minimum wage, without arousing intense passions that border on hatred and bitterness that distorts good judgment. Fear of retribution has shut down debate. Mean-spirited politics has escalated.

The people are not blind to this, but often they feel helpless. Most know that there is a better way—an American way, in fact—for issues to be openly discussed. Instead, political professionals distort the issues to make them sound like violations of deeply held beliefs. In their hands, religious freedom becomes religious suppression. Only with greater understanding and respect can we counteract such deliberate distortions and protect the rights of our citizens.

To make government work we must also make it more accountable to our people. By doing so we will help to restore the confidence of Americans in their government and stimulate the sense of community so necessary to our nation's well-being.

Soaring federal budget deficits have contributed substantially to the growing skepticism about government. President Bush inherited a budget surplus of more than $250 billion and proceeded to plunge the nation back into deficits that exceed $400 billion a year. If the present course continues, the nation will be deep in deficit in coming years, when the baby boom generation begins to retire in 2008 and starts collecting Social Security benefits.

A major part of the problem is the Republican "starve the beast" mentality—the irresponsible mind-set that says the best way to cut federal spending is to cut federal taxes. Reducing taxes is always popular, and Republicans are well aware that it is always difficult and unpopular to raise them again if the reductions are excessive. By reducing taxes, Republicans count on the expectation that the only practical way to rebalance the budget will be to reduce spending, which will reduce the size of government.

The budget process is not working in other ways. A longstanding custom, which has grown explosively in recent years, has allowed individual members of Congress to include funding called earmarks in appropriations bills for special projects in their states, relying on the judgment of the individual members who know the needs of their states best. Some of the projects are worthwhile, others are not, but they are rarely examined closely.

The budget process must be more transparent. Congress should have access to all reasonable information on government finances, especially the likely cost of new programs. The Bush administration unconscionably failed to give Congress the accurate estimate it had made of the cost of the Medicare prescription drug legislation passed in 2004. It even threatened to fire the analyst who prepared the estimate if he divulged that figure before Congress voted.

We must be able to make clear to the American people exactly where their tax dollars are going and what benefits to the nation will result. They should know how much of each federal dollar is used to build the future by investing in national defense and homeland security, in schools and highways, and public transit, and how much goes to vital current benefits such as Social Security and Medicare.

Ending the Culture of Corruption

It is clear that moneyed interests have too much power over candidates. Lobbying is now a multibillion-dollar business. It is hard to find a piece of major legislation that has not been aggressively supported by powerful lobbyists. Most Americans are increasingly distrustful of government because government often seems to speak so little for them. Greater public financing of campaigns is imperative. We already have such financing for presidential elections, and I favor it for Senate and House elections too. At the very least, we need to see that ways to raise funds for candidates' campaigns are untainted so that well-endowed vested interests will not have overwhelming power over candidates and so that successful candidates will be accountable to their constituents, not their financiers.

Congress in recent years has largely abandoned its time-honored responsibility to oversee and review the actions of the executive branch. These oversight functions are an essential part of our system of checks and balances, and they guard against corruption and abuses of power by any president and administration.

But with Republicans in control of Congress there has been little interest in holding the Bush administration accountable in any way for its actions. With only rare exceptions, congressional committees have conducted very few serious investigations and oversight hearings of the White House and cabinet departments. The Republican-led House Government Reform Committee, for example, issued more than a thousand subpoenas to investigate the Clinton administration, but has issued only a hundred to investigate the Bush administration.

In the past, congressional committees would have demanded explanations from the administration for the contracting abuses that hurt our troops in Iraq, for the relaxation of environmental rules on mercury content, for Vice President Cheney's meetings with oil industry executives on energy policy, and for the failing grades that the 9/11 Commission gave to the Department of Homeland Security. It's a sad day for America when any Congress becomes an accomplice in administration cover-ups.

In recent years the nation's business community has been stung by scandal after scandal that form a litany of corruption. The deceit and fraud extended well beyond the dozens of firms themselves to accountants, lawyers, mutual funds, and investment banks. The nation's confidence was shaken. Where was government?

To rebuild confidence we must directly address the integrity of business in America. I remember how quickly our business leaders criticized the financial practices and regulations of Asian economies during the dangerous financial crisis of 1997. But now we know that our own practices have been deceitful and our regulations are inadequate. The free flow of capital is critical to the strength and innovations of American business. It is a practice we cherish, much as we cherish free speech, and like democracy, good business requires the open and honest flow of information under adequate guidelines to ensure that businesses cannot cheat their customers or each other.

Our business sector is too talented to rely on cheating to get ahead. The vast majority of executives are eager to play by the rules and earn profits openly and fairly. But investors, employees, and retirees must be protected from malfeasance. Rules and regulations are vital to the successful functioning and integrity of both private markets and the government.

It is also important to bar the revolving door between government and the private sector. Public officials too readily accept jobs from private sector companies with which they have dealt while in government. The potential for conflict of interest is obvious when agency officials must enforce regulations affecting private firms in which they may soon seek a job. Labor Department officials cannot impartially implement workplace safety requirements at a company that might someday offer them a job. Pentagon officials cannot make objective decisions about weapons purchases if they are seeking jobs with defense contractors. Legislators and staff members in the House and Senate cannot be objective if they plan to join a lobbying firm representing a company that would be affected by proposed bills in their jurisdiction.

We should tighten existing regulations that specify the length of time public officials must wait before going to work for companies they have dealt with. Without effective restrictions on the revolving door between the public and private sectors and on the role of campaign contributions by special interest groups, the culture of corruption will continue to grow and America will be a lesser nation.

Typically, presidents have wide latitude in choosing their staffs. But the Bush administration has used this latitude irresponsibly. The level of incompetence and mismanagement has rarely been equaled in modern times. Congress must accept its full responsibility under the Constitution to fulfill its oversight role of the executive branch. It must demand and the president must provide all necessary information to make responsible decisions on presidential proposals and nominees.

As part of this procedure Congress should insist on full testimony from Cabinet members and other officials on issues of importance—not merely at the time of their nomination but throughout their term of office.

Too often today the executive branch limits the time available for officials to appear before congressional committees to answer direct and vital questions. The use of executive privilege to block the disclosure of information has increasingly been abused. The Bush administration has even sought to limit the availability of the papers of past presidents, and it has repeatedly refused to supply information about its nominees. Congress must demand, and the courts must uphold, the right to adequate information from the executive branch.

In recent years the media have increasingly excused themselves from their responsibility to treat public issues extensively and from diverse points of view. Under President Reagan the legal requirement that radio and television stations present opposing points of view in covering controversial issues—the Fairness Doctrine—was ended. More recently, the Federal Communications Commission has opened the door to the consolidation of the media into a handful of companies. Television and radio stations and magazines and newspapers have been taken over by media conglomerates, and news has been increasingly subjected to the same profitability criteria as automobiles and breakfast cereals.

We need to address these sensitive issues again and make our policy relevant to the information age, always mindful of the constitutional protection of free speech. Survey after survey shows that the public does not trust the press. A renewed fairness doctrine, updated for our times, would require that radio and television provide opposing points of view. Talk radio, for example, is dominated by ideology, usually from the political right. Even the major media, including newspapers and the television network news divisions, too often speak with a timid voice. The Bush administration has used public funds to pay propagandists to act as reporters and write slanted articles for newspapers. Clearly we must reinvigorate the tradition of a free press that serves the public interest, speaks truth to power, and keeps the nation as well informed as possible.

We can unite America behind its basic values only when we show the people that government can work well. Increasing secrecy and deceit in government, a politics of personal destruction and deliberate divisiveness, scandals in business, and incompetence in the management of war abroad and natural disaster at home have led to massive divisions in our nation and a loss of confidence in government. Too often we pass legislation in Congress without understanding how to measure its effectiveness, or have done so with criteria that are ineffective. We too must accept accountability more seriously.

In the end, it is the people who must hold their leaders accountable. They do so by staying informed, by being politically active, by casting their votes. Leadership in turn must listen and respond. When both political parties live up to the nation's truest ideals, we will stand united in America, and America will be back on track.

Afterword

In this book I've outlined a few of the many challenges we face in our country today. I do not underestimate the difficulty of meeting these challenges, but with the right leadership, I'm confident we can face them boldly and successfully. We've done it before, and we can do it again.

I hope this book encourages more Americans to understand the immense importance of these challenges for their own lives and become involved in the debate and cast their votes on Election Day. The genius of our form of government is that it gives the people themselves extraordinary power to create positive change, and they can use that power to put America back on track.

Too many battles have been fought and too much blood has been shed over the years by this great nation for any of us to ignore our right and our solemn obligation to participate in our democracy. Unfortunately, in every presidential election since 1968, fewer than 60 percent of voting-age Americans have cast their votes. In 1996, that number dipped below 50 percent. It is especially troubling that only 50 percent of all Americans in the bottom third of the income distribution voted in 2004 compared to more than 80 percent of those in the top third. To preserve our democracy we must reverse this alarming trend.

In recent years, we have seen tens of millions of people in Eastern Europe, Iraq, Afghanistan, South Africa, and other nations joyously participate in their new democracies by voting in large numbers, many for the first time. Turnout in European elections is routinely higher than in America, and in some nations it exceeds 70 or even 80 percent.

I believe that low voter participation in our nation is a failure of leadership. Year after year for the past quarter century, Republican administrations have aggressively told us what government cannot do. As a result, they have demeaned the power of change that can be achieved through the ballot box. I often hear from young and old alike who feel their vote does not matter. "What difference can my vote make?" they ask. "What change can I make in what government does?" My response is always that their votes can and do make a very real difference, sometimes all the difference. The best way to change the direction of America is to change leaders, and the voting booth is the place to do it.

The policies I have discussed in the preceding chapters are vital to our future. Most of them will pay for themselves. Achieving excellence in education from early childhood through college will return the investment many times over in the form of a higher standard of living for all and a lesser need for social programs. Prevention works in health care, and it can work in other areas as well. Sound policies can again make our nation the most productive and innovative in the world, and make our economy the most inventive and competitive.

Effective health reform will unquestionably reduce the vast sums we now spend for health care and relieve businesses of a growing burden that is reducing their competitiveness in the world economy and making them less willing to hire new employees or pay decent wages.

With an economy that works for all we will stimulate the optimism, energy, and dedication that have made America great from its very beginning. By eliminating bigotry in all its forms and safeguarding the basic rights of our people, we will guarantee genuine equality of opportunity for all, as our Constitution intends, and create a stronger and fairer America.

With better government we will rein in those who are corrupting our democracy and enable government to respond more effectively to the needs of our people. Above all, with better government, with leadership ready, willing, and able to work with other nations to achieve our goals, we can make America safe from violent extremists who thrive in lands where hunger, poverty, and national humiliation are rife. Surely, as President Kennedy told the United Nations in 1961, we can "call a truce to terror" and learn to live together in peace.

Constructing the noble edifice of freedom and democracy has been the supreme and ongoing achievement of our nation ever since "the embattled farmers . . . fired the shot heard round the world." Other lands and other peoples are more than eager to embrace these ideals for their own futures, if only they have the opportunity. America at its best is a brilliant beacon of hope for their aspirations. With leaders who are true to our highest ideals we can resume the march of progress for ourselves and all the world.

Bibliographical Note

The following are many of the key sources I used for this book, and I hope they will provide useful additional information for readers wishing to pursue the issues and ideas raised here.

On early American history, *1776*, by David McCullough (Simon & Schuster, 2005) and *American Sphinx: The Character of Thomas Jefferson*, by Joseph J. Ellis (Alfred A. Knopf, 1997), were particularly valuable. See also Eric Foner, *The Story of American Freedom*, (W. W. Norton, 1998), especially on issues involving the relationship between religion and government. Garry Wills, *Lincoln at Gettysburg: The Words That Remade America* (Simon & Schuster, 1992), vividly describes Lincoln's emphasis on equality as a founding principle of America. On early attitudes toward equality and other principles, see Gordon S. Wood, *The Radicalism of the American Revolution* (Alfred A. Knopf, 1991).

Other important sources on these issues are Sean Wilentz, *The Rise of American Democracy: Jefferson to Lincoln* (W. W. Norton, 2005), and Arthur M. Schlesinger, Jr.'s classic *The Age of Jackson*, first published sixty years ago.

On issues concerning inequality in our democracy today, two excellent sources are the American Political Science Association's *American Democracy in an Age of Rising Inequality* (Task Force on Inequality and American Democracy, 2004) and Richard B. Freeman's essay "What, Me Vote?" in *Social Inequality* (Kathryn M. Neckerman, editor, Russell Sage Foundation Publications, New York, 2004). On party unity in this age of lockstep Republican voting in Congress, see Isaiah J. Poole, "Party Unity Vote Study: Votes

Echo Electoral Themes" (*Congressional Quarterly Weekly*, December 11, 2004). A fine book on Republican tactics is by political scientists Jacob S. Hacker and Paul Pierson, *Off Center: The Republican Party & the Erosion of American Democracy* (Yale University Press, 2005).

Of special value on national security issues are Marc Sageman, "Understanding Terror Networks" (*Foreign Policy Research Institute* (www.fpri.org, 2004); Stephen M. Walt, "Taming American Power" (*Foreign Affairs*, September/October 2005); and General Anthony C. Zinni, Address to the Annual Conference of the Middle East Institute (October 10, 2002).

Excellent sources on weapons of mass destruction are Joseph Cirincione, Jon B. Wolfsthal, and Miriam Rajkumar, *Deadly Arsenals: Nuclear, Biological, and Chemical Threats* (Carnegie Endowment for International Peace, 2005); Sidney Drell and James Goodby, *The Gravest Danger: Nuclear Weapons* (Stanford University Press, 2003); and Matthew Bann and Anthony Weir, *Securing the Bomb 2005: New Global Imperatives* (Harvard University Press and Nuclear Threat Initiative, 2005).

A great deal of valuable economic research has been published on government's role in the economy and the value of public investment. Two recent works summarize the best statistical research on whether government spending or high taxes limit economic growth. See Peter H. Lindert, *Growing Public: Social Spending and Economic Growth Since the Eighteenth Century* (Cambridge University Press, 2004), and Joel B. Slemrod, ed., *Does Atlas Shrug?: The Economic Consequences of Taxing the Rich* (Harvard University Press, 2002). Thoughtful recent works also include Amartya Sen, *Development As Freedom* (Alfred A. Knopf, 1999), and Joseph E. Stiglitz, *The Roaring Nineties: A New History of the World's Most Prosperous Decade* (W. W. Norton, 2003).

A detailed analysis of the economic impact of investment in energy and related public sectors is provided by the Apollo Alliance in *New Energy for America, The Apollo Jobs Report: Good Jobs & Energy Independence* (2004).

An invaluable resource for analysis of income growth and distribution is the biennial report from the Economic Policy Institute by

Lawrence Mishel, Jared Bernstein, and Sylvia Allegretto, *The State of Working America* 2004/2005 (ILR Press).

On America's declining educational quality and international standing, particularly useful information is contained in a study by the National Academies' Committee on Prospering in the Global Economy of the 21st Century, *Rising Above the Gathering Storm: Energizing and Employing America for a Brighter Economic Future* (National Academies Press, 2005).

I consulted numerous studies on education from early childhood through college. An excellent summary of these issues can be found in *Getting Smarter, Becoming Fairer: A Progressive Education Agenda for a Stronger Nation* (Center for American Progress and the Institute for America's Future, 2005). William Bowen and Derek Bok present an impressive analysis of affirmative action in *The Shape of the River* (Princeton University Press, 1998). See also *Empty Promises: The Myth of College Access in America* (Advisory Committee on Student Financial Assistance, 2002), *Trends in College Pricing* (College Board, 2005), and Robert G. Lynch, *Exceptional Returns: Economic, Fiscal, and Social Benefits of Investment in Early Childhood Development* (Economic Policy Institute, 2004).

On racial inequality, a number of impressive sources are available. Of special value is the collection of studies edited by Maria Krysan and Amanda E. Lewis, eds., *The Changing Terrain of Race and Ethnicity* (Russell Sage Foundation Publications, 2004).

On health care issues I relied on numerous sources. On the cost of the lack of insurance in America, see National Academy of Sciences, *Hidden Costs, Value Lost: Uninsurance in America* (National Academies Press, 2003). On quality-of-care issues and the many inadequacies of the current system, an excellent source is David M. Cutler, *Your Money or Your Life: Strong Medicine for America's Health Care System* (Oxford University Press, 2004). For a sophisticated analysis comparing the American system of care to that of other nations, see Peter. S. Hussey, Gerard F. Anderson, Robin Osborn, Colin Feek, Vivienne McLaughlin, John Millar, and Arnold Epstein, "How Does the Quality of Care Compare in Five Countries?"

(Health Affairs, vol. 23, issue 3, 2004). On savings from health information technology, see "HIT Report At-A-Glance" (Department of Health and Human Services, 2004). On the future costs of Medicare, see "2005 Annual Report of the Board of Trustees of Federal Hospital Insurance and Federal Supplementary Medical Insurance Trust Funds." On the cost of health care for all, see Kenneth Thorpe, *Impacts of Health Care Reform: Projections of Costs and Savings,* National Coalition on Health Care, Washington, D.C. (2005).

Index

Adams, John, 184, 187
Affirmative action, 158
Afghanistan, 59
African Americans, discrimination
    against, 153–62
Albright, Madeleine, x
Allegretto, Sylvia, 203
Americans with Disabilities Act, 8,
    42, 166
Anderson, Gerard F., 203
Apollo Alliance, 94

Ball, Robert, x
Bann, Matthew, 202
Bernstein, Jared, 203
Best medical practices, 135–37
Bin Laden, Osama, 59, 60, 64
Blix, Hans, 182
Bok, Derek, 158
Bolton, John, 33
Bowen, William G., 158
Bradford, William, 10
Brown v. Board of Education, 6, 150
Budget process, 191–92
Bush, George H. W., 37, 67, 116, 185
Bush, George W., 22, 29, 38, 40, 42,
    65, 87, 96, 109–10, 111, 119,
    152, 157, 189, 190
Business scandals, 193–94

Bybee, Jay, 37, 38

Caper, Philip, x
Carter, Jimmy, 67
Character assassinations, 187
Checks and balances, 20–21, 22–27,
    40–43, 192
Cheney, Dick, 24, 32, 193
Churchill, Winston, ix
Cirincione, Joseph, 202
Civil Rights Act (1964), 6–7, 150
Clarke, Richard, 182
Cleland, Max, 188
Clinton, Bill, 32–33, 37, 67, 105,
    109, 119–20, 122, 140, 178–79
College enrollment, enhancing,
    88–89
Communications infrastructure, 95
Community, spirit of, 174, 183–92
Conflicts of interest, public officials
    and, 194–95
Congress
    executive actions, review of,
      192–93
    thwarting role of, 20–21, 22–27
Constitutional democracy, reclaim-
    ing of, 14–15, 18–44
    checks and balances, abuse of. *See*
      Checks and balances

(Const'l democ. cont'd)
Congress, thwarting role of,
20–21, 22–27
judicial branch, independence of,
40–44
presidential war powers, 28
privacy, 43–44
secrecy, 27–36, 40
Corporations
burden of providing health care
coverage by, 140–41
inadequacy of health care coverage, 137–39
scandals, 193–94
Cutler, David M., 203

DeLay, Tom, 25–26
Dirksen, Everett, 7
Disabled persons, discrimination
against, 165–66
Discrimination
against disabled persons, 165–66
against gays and lesbians, 166–68
gender, 162–65
housing, 156
racial, 153–62
sexual, 166–68
against women, 162–65
Drell, Sidney, 202
Dulles, John Foster, 55

Early childhood education, revitalization of, 82–84
Economic equality, 16, 102–27
level of, 105–8
minimum wage, 110–16
pensions, 125
retirement income, security of,
122–26
strengthening economy, 109–10
taxation, 118–20
unionization, 116–18

workplace laws, modernization of,
121–23
Education
college enrollment, enhancing,
88–89
early childhood, 82–84
equal opportunity in, 156–58
No Child Left Behind Act, 87, 157
public, 85–88
revitalization of, 77–82
segregation in, 157–58
Eisenhower, Dwight D., 55, 116,
124
ElBaradei, Mohammed, 67, 182
Ellis, Joseph J., 201
Employer-based health care coverage, inadequacy of, 138–40
Energy conservation, 91–94
Energy task force, 32–33
Epstein, Arnold, 203
Equality, economic. *See* Economic
equality
Equal opportunity, 16, 149–73
affirmative action, 158
civil rights acts. *See* specific acts
discrimination. *See* Discrimination
education, 156–58
hunger, 169–71
immigrants, 171–73
poverty, 170–71
Estrada, Miguel, 33
Executive actions, restoring congressional review of, 192–93

Fair Housing Act, 7, 151
Family and Medical Leave Act,
163–64
Federal Emergency Management
Agency (FEMA)
Hurricane Katrina failure, 65–66,
180
mismanagement of, 180–81

"Federalist 51," 28–29
Feek, Colin, 203
FEMA. *See* Federal Emergency
    Management Agency (FEMA)
FISA. *See* Foreign Intelligence Sur-
    veillance Act (FISA)
Fitzgerald, John F. ("Honey Fitz"),
    2–4, 187
Foner, Eric, 201
Ford, Gerald, 67, 116
Foreign Intelligence Surveillance
    Act (FISA), 22
Foreign policy framework, develop-
    ment of new, 58–63
Foster, Richard, 33–34
Franklin, Benjamin, 20
Freeman, Richard B., 201

Gates, Bill, 139
Gays and lesbians, discrimination
    against, 166–68
Gender discrimination, 162–65
Glenmullen, Joseph, 34
Globalization, 15–16, 71–101
    college enrollment, enhancing,
        88–89
    early childhood education, revital-
        ization of, 82–84
    education, revitalization of, 77–82
    energy conservation, 91–94
    history of, 75–76
    job training, 89–91
    offshoring of jobs, 97–101
    public education system, 85–88
    research and development, 95–97
    response to, 74–75
    technology, 76–77
Gonzales, Alberto, 33, 37–38, 39
Goodby, James, 202
Government
    benefits of, 176–77
    business scandals and, 193–94
    conflicts of interest, 194–95
    congressional review of executive
        actions, restoring, 192–93
    distrust of, 179–83
    faith in, restoring, 183–92
    media coverage of, 195–97
    as partner in economy, 175–80
    presidential appointees, accounta-
        bility of, 195
    private sector companies, public
        officials accepting jobs with,
        194–95
    regulation, 175
Gramm, Phil, 178

Hacker, Jacob S., 202
Hamburg, David, 83
Hamilton, Kendall, 166–67
Hamilton, Lee, 30–31
Hart, Phil, 7
Hate crimes, 167–68
Havel, Václav, 185
Head Start, 84
Health care, 16, 127–48
    best medical practices, 135–37
    complexities of system, 141–44
    corporations, burden on, 140–41
    costs of current system, 141–44
    employer-based coverage, inade-
        quacy of, 138–40
    goals of, 131–33
    high costs of, 130–31
    Medicare. *See* Medicare
    plan to improve system, 145–48
    preventive medicine, 132–35, 147
    uninsured persons, 137–38
    universal coverage, 146–47
Helms, Jesse, 37
Himmelstein, David, 139
Homeland security, 65–66
Honey Fitz. *See* Fitzgerald, John F.
Hoover, Herbert, 16, 188

Housing discrimination, 156
Humphrey, Hubert, 7
Hunger in America, 168–70
Hurricane Katrina, 65–66, 91–92, 110–11, 180
Hussein, Saddam, 36, 38, 59, 60, 68, 69, 183
Hussey, Peter S., 203

Immigration, 171–73
International cooperation, 99–101
Iraq war
    damage caused by, 68–69
    intelligence briefings, 31–32
    mistakes leading to, 59–61
    prewar intelligence, 29
    War on Terror, effect on, 61–62

Jefferson, Thomas, 183–84, 185–86, 187, 189
Job training, 89–91, 98–99
Johnson, Frank M., 7
Johnson, Lyndon B., 7, 10, 67, 150, 171, 177, 179
Judicial branch, independence of, 40–44

Katzenbach, Nicholas, 7
Kean, Thomas, 30–31
Kelly, Eamon, x
Kennedy, Edward M., Jr., 128
Kennedy, John F., 5, 7, 10, 11, 55, 60, 63, 70, 103, 127, 150, 177, 179, 187, 188, 200
Kennedy, Joseph P., Jr., 127
Kennedy, Kara, 128
Kennedy, Patrick, 128
Kennedy, Robert F., 7, 55, 160
Kennedy, Rosemary, 127
Kennedy, Vicki, x
Kerry, John, 188
Keynes, John Maynard, 75

Khrushchev, Nikita, 10
King, Martin Luther, Jr., 6, 7, 151
Koh, Harold, x, 38
Krysan, Maria, 203

Lewis, Amanda E., 203
Lincoln, Abraham, 1, 184, 185
Lindert, Peter, 202
Lobbyists, 188–89
Lodge, George Cabot, 186, 188
Lodge, Henry Cabot, Jr., 188
Lodge, Henry Cabot, Sr., 187
Loy, James (Adm.), 65
Lynch, Robert G., 203

McCain, John, 39, 172, 188
McCormack, Edward J., 186
McCormack, John W., 186
McCullough, David, 201
McLaughlin, Vivienne, 203
Mansfield, Mike, 7
Marshall, Burke, 7
Marshall, John, 19
Media, 195–97
Medicare, 8–9, 23–24, 142
    plan to expand, 145–46
    prescription drug plan, 33–34
Medicare for All, 133
Melville, Herman, 102
Millar, John, 203
Minimum wage, 110–16
Minorities, equal opportunity for.
    See Equal opportunity
Mishel, Lawrence, 203
Moral authority, 48–49
Morrison, Steve, 167
Murtha, John, 188

Nash, William (Gen.), x
National security, 15, 45–70
    concerns, 50–51
    damage done to, 68–69

homeland security, 65–66
lessons from past, 56–58
new definition of, 49–52
new foreign policy framework,
  development of, 58–63
nuclear nonproliferation, 66–68
National Security Strategy, Bush
  administration, 53–56
Nixon, Richard M., 67, 124, 151
No Child Left Behind Act, 87, 157
Nuclear nonproliferation, 66–68

O'Connor, Sandra Day, 42
Offshoring of jobs, 97–101
Osborn, Robin, 203
Overtime, 121–22

Peace Corps, 11
Pell, Claiborne, 37
Pensions, 125
Perry, William, x
Perry Pre-School Program, 83–84
Pierson, Paul, 202
Plame, Valerie, 35, 182
Poole, Isaiah, J., 201
Poverty, 111–12, 170–71
Powell, Colin, 59
Prescription drug plan, Medicare,
  33–34
Presidential appointees, accounta-
  bility of, 195
Preventive medicine, 133–37, 147
Preventive war, 49, 52–56
Privacy, 43–44
Private sector companies, public
  officials accepting jobs with,
  194–95
Public education, revitalization of,
  85–88

Racial discrimination, 153–62
Rajkumar, Miriam, 202

Reagan, Ronald, 36, 38, 67, 108,
  121, 124, 152, 174, 195–96
Redistricting plan, Texas, 25–26
Rehabilitation Act, 8
Rehnquist, William H., 40–41
Reich, Robert, x
Religion, 4–5, 188
Research and development, 95–97
Respect for America, 47–48
Retirement income, security of,
  122–26
Romero, Anthony, x
Romney, Mitt, 187
Roosevelt, Franklin D., 41, 63, 76,
  103, 111, 116, 117, 123, 142
Roosevelt, Theodore, 118
Rubin, Robert, 120

Safety net, expansion of worker,
  98–99
Sageman, Marc, 202
Schlesinger, Arthur M., Jr., 201
Secrecy, 27–36, 40
Sen, Amartya, 202
September 11 terrorist attacks, 45,
  47
Sexual discrimination, 166–68
Shinseki, Eric (Gen.), 35, 182
Shrinking world. *See* Globalization
Shriver, Sargent R., 11
Slemrod, Joel B., 202
Smith, Al, 188
Social Security, 123–25
Spirit of community, 174
Steinberg, James, x
Stiglitz, Joseph E., 202
Supreme Court, 40–44

Taxation, 118–20
Tax cuts, 109–10, 119–20
Terrorism, 45–70. *See also* War on
  Terror

Texas redistricting plan, 25–26
Thorpe, Kenneth, 204
Title IX, 165
Tocqueville, Alexis de, 43, 102
Torture, 36–40
Transportation policy, 94
Truman, Harry S., 54, 55, 63, 149
Tyson, Laura D'Andrea, 140–41

Unemployment insurance, 120–21
Uninsured persons, 137–38
Unionization, 116–18

Values, 17, 174–97
vanden Heuvel, William, x
Voting Rights Act, 150–51
    violation of, 152

Walt, Stephen M., x, 202
Warren, Earl, 7
War on Terror, 46

Iraq war, effect of, 61–62
    strategy for winning, 63–65
Whistle blowers, 34–35
White, Byron, 7
Wilentz, Sean, 201
Wills, Garry, 201
Wilson, Joseph, 34–35, 181, 182
Wilson, Woodrow, 63, 187
Wisdom, John Minor, 7
Wofford, Harris, 7
Wolfstahl, Jon B., 202
Women, discrimination against,
    162–65
Wood, Gordon, 102, 201
Workplace laws, modernization of,
    121–23
Wright, J. Skelly, 7

Yoo, John, 38

Zinni, Anthony (Gen.), x, 202